The TRUTH *About...*

Addressing Today's Problems
with Bible Answers

Don Blackwell

Produced and published by:

World Video Bible School®
25 Lantana Lane
Maxwell, Texas 78656
www.WVBS.org

Copyright © **2014**

ISBN: 978-0-9894311-2-5

Artwork: Mat Cain | Layout Design: Branyon May and Chris Fisher

Special Thanks:

I would like to express sincere thanks to several people who put a great deal of effort into making this book a reality. First, thanks to Lacey Deaver and her efforts in rewriting my scripts. Thanks to Rod Rutherford, Loretta Horner and Carol Anne Braswell and their editorial expertise. Thanks to Rudy Cain for making this project a reality and his great vision in the Lord's kingdom. Special thanks to my good friend Branyon May for the countless hours he has put in doing the layout of the book. My prayer is that much good will come as a result. ~Don Blackwell

Serving the Church since 1986

wvbs.org

Table of Contents

Foreword

I am happy to commend this excellent and timely book on moral issues by Don Blackwell. Don is one of the finest of the younger generation of preachers in the brotherhood today. He is sound in doctrine and life, scholarly in approach and powerful in proclamation of the truth of the gospel. It has been my privilege to be associated with Don on several occasions in the Lord's work. I have always been impressed by his zeal, ability, integrity and the thoroughness with which he handles any assignment.

Don addresses several key moral issues facing not only young people, but every member of the Lord's church. I believe this book is a "must read" for teenagers as well as for their parents and the teachers who work with them. It is a valuable resource for preachers as well. It is my recommendation that every congregation have a class covering the subjects dealt with so ably by Don in this book. Preachers would also do well to preach a series on these topics to the entire congregation. They will find much helpful, factual material in the book. Each lesson can easily be made into a sermon or lesson outline.

Rod Rutherford
Gatlinburg, Tennessee

Dedication

This book is dedicated to my sweet and supportive wife, Sheri, who is one who certainly does not need to read it. She has been supportive of me in my every endeavor, and I'm a better person because of her. She loves the Lord more than anything in the world, which is what makes her such a treasure.

Tattoos and Piercings

It's nearly impossible to go out in public these days without seeing someone with a tattoo or body piercing. The movie stars have them. The sports figures have them. In fact, a news story dated April 30, 2009 says that Barbie now has them. In celebration of the fiftieth anniversary of the Barbie doll, Mattel has created a new Barbie, complete with tattoos and a toy tattoo gun so children can stamp themselves with washable tattoos.[1] The American Academy of Dermatology website says that 24 percent of people 18 to 50 reported having a tattoo.[2] A Harris Poll dated February 12, 2008, stated that 32 percent of those aged 25 to 29 had a tattoo, and 25 percent of people 30 to 39 had them.[3] Because tattoos and piercings are so popular, it's a topic young people have to deal with and about which they naturally have many questions. "Is it right for a Christian to get a tattoo?" "Is it right to have multiple piercings in your ears? What about a ring in your nose?"

Parents don't always know how best to answer these questions. Sometimes Christian parents who discuss these things with their children aren't sure if the issues really matter. Are these things matters of right and wrong or just purely matters of opinion? What does the Bible say? Does it even address these issues?

We want to be fair in answering these questions. We don't want to misuse the Scriptures in any way or reach unwarranted conclusions. Neither is it our goal to shame or embarrass anyone. We want to examine this topic in light of relevant Bible passages and then draw accurate conclusions based on what God says on the matter.

Tattoos

MISCONCEPTIONS

Frequently when discussing the subject of tattoos or body piercings, someone might argue, "The Bible specifically forbids them." The fact is there is no passage in the Bible that says, "Thou shalt not get a tattoo." Many times people will cite Leviticus 19:28, believing that it addresses our question. It states, "You shall not make any cuttings on your flesh for the dead, nor tattoo any marks on you: I am the LORD." This is actually not a proper use of this passage. First, we have to be very careful about trying to use an Old Testament passage as a proof text to regulate activities in the New Testament Christian Age. The Law of Moses was nailed to the cross, and it is not the standard by which we live today. Notice also the same chapter which forbids putting marks on one's body also gives instructions concerning animal sacrifices. It also requires leaving certain portions of one's crops unharvested, forbids sowing two types of seed in the same field, and tells the Hebrews they were not to wear a garment with two different types of fabric (wool and linen). There are restrictions about how a man's hair was to be cut and prohibitions as to how he could trim his beard. Are we behaving fairly when we bind just one of these restrictions? Certainly not.

The context of Leviticus 19:27-28 is that of avoiding heathen practices and things associated with idolatry. "Cutting the flesh" is mentioned. In 1 Kings 18:28 the prophets of Baal cut themselves in efforts to elicit a response from their god. Archeological evidence shows that some of the Canaanites tattooed themselves with the names or symbols of their favorite gods. Idolatry is probably what God is prohibiting in His injunction against cutting the flesh, not the modern practice of tattoos. Christians should be careful not to create invalid arguments when pulling passages from the Bible. False reasoning not only invalidates the case we are trying to make but also hurts our credibility. When we use such arguments, we are not rightly handling the word of truth. There *is* the principle in Leviticus 19 that we are not to associate ourselves with ungodly things, but that would be all we could draw from the passage.

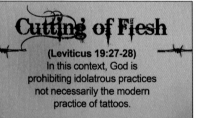

Cutting of Flesh
(Leviticus 19:27-28)
In this context, God is prohibiting idolatrous practices not necessarily the modern practice of tattoos.

So we must conclude that there is no Bible passage that says, "Thou shalt not get a tattoo."

However, just because there is no direct prohibition against tattoos doesn't necessarily mean that it's right to get one. There is no passage in the Bible saying, "Thou shalt not inject heroin into thy veins," but we understand that it's wrong because of biblical principles. So in determining if an activity is right or wrong, a Christian needs to ask himself certain questions, such as what would this do to my influence? Would this be a stumbling block for others? Is engaging in this practice good stewardship? Will this have negative effects on me as a servant of God?

BIBLICAL PRINCIPLES

#1 The Principle of INFLUENCE

Let's begin by examining a passage in 1 Corinthians 11. A rather unusual discussion takes place in this chapter concerning the wearing of veils. The apostle Paul writes, "But every woman who prays or prophesies with her head uncovered dishonors her head, for that is one and the same as if her head were shaved" (11:5). Verse 6 goes on to say, "For if a woman is not covered, let her also be shorn. But if it is shameful for a woman to be shorn or shaved, let her be covered."

Some believe this passage mandates a woman's wearing of a veil in worship at all times. That conclusion is not correct. In fact, Paul is quite clear in verse 16: "But if anyone seems to be contentious, we have no such custom, nor do the churches of God." If the point of the passage is not that women for all time must wear a veil, then why does Paul command the women in Corinth to do so? The answer is simple. When Paul was writing to the church in Corinth, it was customary for a woman to wear a veil: not to wear one was a sign of rejecting the husband's authority. That culture would find that very offensive. No Christian woman wanted to leave that impression.

What connection does this have with tattoos?

In our current society, tattoos send a particular message. For years they have been associated with a counter-culture. Tattoos (and unusual body piercings) send a message of a certain type of person, and they are associated with a certain type of people.

A former policeman reflected on the time of his career when more and more officers began acquiring tattoos. The department issued a new policy: officers could get tattoos only if they were hidden by their uniforms. The reason? Because of the message tattoos send. Numerous news stories on the Internet discuss the problem of tattoos and body piercings in the workplace. One article from Fox News points out that some employers are having to write very specific dress codes to address the problem.[4] Many employers are requiring that their staff dress in such a way as to hide their tattoos.

The new tattoo Barbie doll was mentioned earlier. Here is an excerpt from an article discussing this new doll:[1]

"Parents have already rallied up against Mattel, asking for the dolls to be pulled off the market."

One parent asked, "Whatever will they bring out next? Drug addict Barbie? Alcoholic Barbie?" Why are parents rallying against Mattel? Because in our society tattoos have negative connotations.

A Native American man named Apache Crying Bear has tattoos all over his body. He worked for many years as a professional tattoo artist. Apache says, "Police and judges look at you differently."

Apache can hardly find a job because of his tattoos. People don't view him in the same light as if he had no tattoos.

What does all this have to do with 1 Corinthians 11? The principle is that society's view of an issue can make its practice sinful for a Christian. If society views not wearing a veil as rebellious and overstepping one's bounds, then a Christian should not do it. In that light, if we conclude that Christians having tattoos or excessive piercings are considered rebellious or associated with sin, then without a doubt Christians should avoid them. Otherwise, they will hurt their influence and the influence of the church.

On the subject of influence, let us consider also that many times the places a person has to go to get a tattoo will be harmful to his or her influence. Going into a bar is wrong even if one doesn't drink. Going into a strip club is wrong even if one doesn't look. Going into a casino is wrong even if one doesn't gamble. Why? Because those practices are very destructive to one's influence.

What about tattoo parlors? Generally speaking, they have very seedy reputations. Sometimes their names alone speak volumes:

- Sinful Inflictions
- Dark Images
- Red Devil Tattoo and Piercing

It is disturbing how many tattoo and piercing parlors have the word *sinful* in their names.

#2 The Principle of MODESTY

The point being made here is not what you might think. Although it could be related, this is not in reference to showing too much skin. Rather, we are referring to a word that appears in the Bible in 1 Timothy 2:9-10. It says, "In like manner also, that women adorn themselves in modest apparel, with shamefacedness and sobriety; not with braided hair, or gold, or pearls, or costly array; but which becometh women professing godliness with good works."

Let us consider four words and phrases in this text. First is the word *modest*. It means "orderly, well-arranged, or decent." The idea is that this woman is not to adorn (beautify) herself in a way that draws undue attention to herself. In the immediate context, Paul is discussing a woman *overdoing* it—wearing flashy clothes, lots of makeup, and expensive jewelry.

Of course, a woman could also draw undue attention to herself by *underdoing* it, that is, by wearing too little. But consider this statement in light of the "tattoo and body piercing" discussion. Can we draw undue attention to ourselves with tattoos, nose rings, or navel piercings? Of course we can!

The second word to consider from this passage is *shamefacedness*. Shamefacedness is actually closer to our modern word *modest* than the first word we discussed. The Greek word for *shamefacedness*

Modesty

Can we draw undue attention to ourselves with tattoos, nose rings, or navel piercings?

means, "a sense of shame, modesty."

The third word is *sobriety*. When we think of sobriety, we usually think of alcohol. That is because sobriety relates to being sober, not having the senses and judgment dulled by alcohol. In the original language, sobriety carried with it the idea of "soundness of mind and self-control." It speaks of a person who is exercising good judgment.

The fourth thing to take from this passage is the phrase in verse 10: "which becometh women professing godliness." In other words, "in a manner that says to the world, *I am a servant of God*. My most important concern is to be godly."

Let's pull all of this together and see what we have. Christians are to adorn (decorate) themselves in a way that does not draw undue attention to themselves. They should have a sense of shame and modesty about them. They ought to exercise good judgment; they are to dress and adorn themselves so as to communicate godliness. Do tattoos communicate godliness? What about a stud in one's tongue? Does that show a sense of shame and good judgment? Is that what people conclude when they see a person with multiple tattoos and piercings?

There is a particular type of tattoo that has been very popular in recent years. It is typically worn by women and is placed at the base of their back so that when their shirt raises, the observer's eye is drawn to that part of the body. That specific tattoo is commonly known as a "tramp stamp." In light of what Paul says in 1 Timothy 2, a person would have to admit that such a tattoo does not mesh with godly principles.

#3 The Principle of STEWARDSHIP

The two points to think about under this principle are the stewardship of our bodies and the stewardship of our money. Before you reject the stewardship argument as weak, think about the risks and consider the stewardship of your body.

The Mayo Clinic website states,[5]

"Tattoo inks are classified as cosmetics, so they aren't regulated or approved by the Food and Drug Administration (FDA). The pigments and dyes used in tattoo inks aren't

approved for injection under the skin. Long-term effects of these are unknown."

The site also lists some of the specific risks associated with getting a tattoo.

First there are the blood-borne diseases, including:

- Hepatitis C
- Hepatitis B
- Tetanus
- Tuberculosis
- HIV

In continuing to list the risks of tattoos, the Mayo Clinic also mentions "skin disorders, skin infections, allergic reactions, and on rare occasions they can even cause problems when a person needs to get an MRI."

According to Apache Crying Bear, there are hundreds of infection possibilities involved in getting a tattoo. Apache says he personally knew of cases where 2,500 people fell victim to Hepatitis C after getting a tattoo. Some of the dangers involved in getting a tattoo are the same for body piercings. Somebody might say, "I go to a clean, upscale tattoo parlor." In all actuality, tattooists are not doctors, and each place is going to claim it is a clean, upscale establishment in order to win more customers.

All of this does not consider the *pain* associated with getting a tattoo. In addition, there are long-term effects such as disfigurement. Over time tattoos stretch, fade, and began to look very bad. Then, too, there is the regret factor. For various reasons, many people who get tattoos look back years later, or maybe even soon afterward, and regret their body marking that will be there the rest of their lives. What is cool to a teenager does not have the same vibe to a 40-year-old.

Stewardship of our bodies is only one issue to consider. The second is the stewardship of our money. Someone may argue, "It's my money and I can buy whatever I want with it." But that isn't really true. Our money belongs to God, and we're just stewards of what He gives us.

Someone else might say, "Well, it's not wrong to purchase things we enjoy. Maybe you spend money for movie tickets or an iPod, but I choose to spend mine on a tattoo."

We agree that it is not wrong to spend money on recreation and pleasurable activities, but when we do that we must always consider the stewardship principles. Depending on one's personal financial situation, bills and the amount of money one should be giving to the Lord, it may be that buying that iPod is not appropriate at the time. It may mean that buying a new car right now might be poor stewardship. So the stewardship principle is one that everyone needs to consider carefully. We must weigh it and draw appropriate conclusions.

Tattoos can be very expensive. A person needs to ask himself, "Is this a wise use of my money?" "Will the Lord be pleased if I spend my money this way?"

According to Bill Johnson, the executive office director of the Alliance of Professional Tattooists, most tattoo artists charge an

hourly rate that varies from about 75 to 150 dollars. The process will take from one to several hours, depending on the size and complexity of the tattoo.[6] In addition, some tattoo artists charge 10 to 25 percent extra if the tattoo is on a more difficult part of the body. When a person comes to regret his tattoo, having it removed is even more expensive than getting it. Removal requires from 5 to 20 sessions at a cost of 200 to 500 dollars per session. If you calculate that, someone getting a tattoo removed could be looking at ten thousand dollars, along with the pain associated with it.[6] Laser tattoo removal has been compared to being splattered with hot grease, so some choose to have a local anesthetic, which only increases the cost.[6]

Someone might ask, "What if I only want to get one tattoo, and it's something innocent, like a butterfly or something?"

There are several factors that would influence the effects of having a tattoo: where on one's body the tattoo is located; how many tattoos one has; what the tattoo's design is. All of these things are going to affect how people look at you. For example, a tattoo of a butterfly is not going to be viewed the same way as a tattoo of a skull and crossbones or a black widow spider.

Regardless, there are certain negative connotations associated with tattoos, and 1 Timothy 5:14 speaks about "not giving occasion to the adversary to speak reproachfully." A person is still going to have to go into a tattoo parlor to get one. One still runs the risk of infections and diseases from bad needles. One still has to deal with the principles of modesty and good judgment in 1 Timothy 2.

Another question someone may put forth is, "What about getting a religious tattoo, perhaps a cross or something to profess my faith?"

Remember there are many very ungodly people who have tattoos. Having a tattoo of a cross is not necessarily going to set you apart. In fact, having a tattoo is going to make you more like them. What does it say about you as a Christian when you have a tattoo?

Here's a third question: "What if I already have tattoos?"

For someone who already has a tattoo, our discussion might make them feel very self-conscious. We are not trying to embarrass anyone. We want people to examine Christian principles and then make decisions that are the most in line with the Bible. If you have excessive body piercings, you can change that. If you have a ring in your nose, you can take it out. But if you already have a tattoo, there is not much you can do about it short of spending a great deal of money to have it removed. One Christian

> **Already have a Tattoo?**
> Don't let it violate the principles of **Influence & Modesty**. Don't let it stop you from being a **faithful Christian**.

put it this way: "When I became a Christian, baptism washed away my sins but it didn't wash away my tattoo." That is true, but it doesn't mean someone with a tattoo cannot be called a faithful Christian.

IN CONCLUSION

Tattoos and excessive body piercings can hurt and perhaps even destroy a person's influence. They can violate principles of modesty. They can pose grave risks to one's health, and they may result in poor stewardship. But if you already have them, it is not too late. They cannot stop you from serving the Lord and being a faithful Christian.

Each of us should have the attitude of the apostle Paul: "I am crucified with Christ: nevertheless I live; yet not I, but Christ liveth in me" (Galatians 2:20). Why? Because Jesus said, "If any man will come after me, let him *deny himself*, and take up his cross and follow me" (Matthew 16:24). We are to live for the Lord, and as 1 Timothy 5:14 says, we don't want to give any occasion to the adversary to speak reproachfully.

Video Resources

THE TRUTH ABOUT... TATTOOS & PIERCINGS

This video covers the controversial topic of modern tattoos and piercings. How should Christians view tattoos and piercings?

TheTruthAbout.net/video/Tattoos-Piercings

Gambling! Is it an innocent pastime, a way to fund education and help our community, an extra source of income? Or is it something with far-reaching consequences? Is it merely a recreational activity, or a serious moral problem?

Some people think gambling is acceptable to God and some think it's wrong. People have gone to the Scriptures seeking answers, but they say, "I can't find a single verse that addresses the topic."

It is true that there is no verse in the Bible that says, "Thou shalt not play Blackjack," but it is not the case that the Bible does not address gambling.

The Bible does indeed teach that gambling is wrong. Let's look at several principles that deal with the issue, because arguments for gambling are very weak. People say, "Gambling is wrong because the Bible teaches us that we are to work for our money." That is true. We are to work and make a living, but if that argument was taken at face value, giving and receiving gifts would be sinful. It would also be sinful for Christians to assist the poor and for the poor to accept help from the church.

Someone might also say, "Gambling is wrong because of the risk factor." That is not true. Risk in and of itself is not wrong. Life is a risk. When a man gets into his car to go to work, he is taking a risk. Being a Christian is a risk. That was especially so in the first century. In Matthew 25, the man with one talent was condemned because he wouldn't take a risk. When a farmer plants his crops, he is taking a risk. When a man buys stock, he is taking a risk. So we can easily see that the risk factor alone is not that which makes something sinful. As Christians, we have to be very careful about our arguments. Truth suffers when we make weak or inadequate arguments.

Let's begin with the definition of gambling. What are we talking about? There are three basic elements of gambling: (1) An uncertain, arbitrary event; (2) the wager, something of value, such as money, that is deliberately chanced on a particular outcome; and (3) a winner and a loser. The winner is financially benefited by the direct loss of someone else. When all three factors merge, the result is gambling.

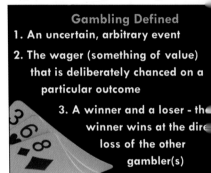

Gambling Defined
1. An uncertain, arbitrary event
2. The wager (something of value) that is deliberately chanced on a particular outcome
3. A winner and a loser - the winner wins at the dire loss of the other gambler(s)

BIBLICAL REASONING FOR WHY GAMBLING IS WRONG

Reason #1: COVETOUSNESS

What motivates people to gamble? Think about that for a minute. Two things immediately come to mind: greed and covetousness.

Under the Law of Moses, one of the Ten Commandments was, "Thou shalt not covet." That means don't lust after, long for, or desire something that belongs to somebody else. Exodus 20:17 says, "You shall not covet your neighbor's house; you shall not covet your neighbor's wife, nor his male servant, nor his female servant, nor his ox, nor his donkey, nor anything that is your neighbor's." What about his money lying on the table? How does one sit around the table and gamble over a poker game without violating this principle? Notice that this principle also applies to the New Law under which we live. In Luke 12:15 Jesus said, "Take heed and beware of covetousness, for one's life does not consist in the abundance of the things he possesses."

Why is gambling wrong? Because of what motivates man to do it.

Reason #2: IT PREYS ON THE WEAKNESS OF OTHERS

Christian principles are just the opposite of this. Christian principles teach, "As we have opportunity, let us do good to all..." (Galatians 6:10). That means helping those in need, not taking their money. Biblical principles teach us to help the poor and feed the hungry. Gambling steals from the poor and robs the hungry.

The busiest day in Atlantic City casinos is the day after welfare checks hit the mailboxes. People who can't afford to lose their money are in the casinos, hoping to strike it rich. A gambler may win at the loss of one who can least afford to lose. A disproportionate number of people who play the lottery are the very poor. They take food out of their children's mouths in hopes of winning the lottery. In fact, one study found that "the poor bet approximately three times the amount wagered by persons in middle-income and upper-income areas."[1] While another study concluded that "the lotteries in Connecticut and Massachusetts were equivalent to a state sales tax of over 60 percent on lower-income groups. Gambling preys on the weaknesses of others."[1] It profits at the pain of others. It is exactly the opposite of what Christianity teaches.

Reason #3: THE FRUIT TEST

In Matthew 7:15-20, Jesus Christ laid down a test by which every activity or philosophy could be measured. He said, "Every good tree bears good fruit, but a bad tree bears bad fruit. A good tree cannot bear bad fruit, nor can a bad tree bear good fruit." This passage was spoken about false teachers, but the principle is certainly true with regard to activities in life.

Let's ask this question: "What kind of fruit does gambling produce?" When legalized gambling arrives in a new community, does it raise the moral standards of that community? Does it help to lessen the hardships of families in that area? No, it does just the opposite. Many times, if you drive into a state with legalized gambling—whether it be a lottery or a casino-filled strip—you can see the faces of ten-million-dollar winners smiling brightly on roadside billboards. You might think, "That's a good thing!" But the reality is vastly different than what the brightly smiling winners portray. Gambling does not pass the fruit test.

Eight months after casinos opened in Gulfport, Mississippi, the Gulfport Police Department noted the following: murder increased by 75 percent; rape increased by 200 percent; robbery increased by 311 percent; assaults increased by 64 percent; burglary increased by 100 percent; and vehicle theft increased by 160 percent.[2]

Only three years after casinos arrived, Atlantic City shot from fiftieth to first in per-capita crime. And what about Las

Vegas, which is probably the gambling capital of the United States? Some statistical studies show that Nevada ranks first in suicide, first in divorce, first in high school dropouts, first in homicide against women, first in gambling addictions, third in bankruptcies, third in abortion, fourth in rape, fourth in out-of-wedlock births, fourth in alcohol-related deaths, fifth in crime, sixth in the number of prisoners locked up, and last in voter participation.[2]

Someone might say, "Well, that may not all be due to gambling. They have prostitution and drinking, and other things that may be contributing factors." That isn't to be doubted, but isn't it interesting how these things go together? These statistics show a completely different billboard from the roadside sign mentioned a moment ago. It is easy to see how gambling fails the fruit test!

Reason #4: PROVERBS 13:11

People sometimes say there aren't any verses in the Bible dealing with gambling, but there's actually a very interesting verse in Proverbs 13:11. The King James renders it: "Wealth

GAMBLING

gotten by vanity shall be diminished, but he that gathereth by labour shall increase."

The word *vanity* here means "emptiness, nothingness." Does wealth gotten by emptiness sound like gambling? The English Standard Version says, "Wealth gained hastily will dwindle." But the footnote reads, "wealth gained by fraud." This too sounds like gambling. Another translation says, "Wealth gotten from get-rich-quick schemes quickly disappears; wealth from hard work grows." Still another translation says, "Wealth from gambling quickly disappears; wealth from hard work grows."

There undoubtedly are principles in this particular verse which directly reflect on gambling in a negative way.

Reason #5: THE ADDICTION OF GAMBLING

There should be no doubts about gambling being addictive. When people win at gambling, they want to win again. They want more. Their greed and covetousness often spiral out of control until it takes over their lives. When people *lose* at gambling, they want to win back what they have lost. It's addictive!

The *Nevada Observer* references one very interesting piece of information from the Center on Budget and Policy Priorities. It refers to gambling as being recession proof. In other words, people gamble even when they can't afford it. Gambling is addictive.

So many people have fallen prey to the gambling addiction that we have organizations in the United States, such as Gambler's Anonymous, to help addicts deal with their problem. One Texas preacher stated that on the back of lottery tickets, there was a phone number for the gambler's help line. I don't know if that is currently true, but isn't it interesting? That preacher called and requested information. According to the information he received, the biggest gambling problem in Texas was the lottery. It led with 73 percent.

In the *Christian Courier*, Wayne Jackson cites one study revealing that 43 percent of those who gamble have a tendency toward compulsion that results in their spending more money than they can afford. Some years ago, an online article that referenced the *Dallas Times Herald*, told of a pawn shop owner who had patrons who sold him their artificial limbs. In one case, a glass eye, in another case, gold teeth pulled out with pliers and hocked for money with which to gamble. Now that is addiction! In 1 Corinthians 6:12 the apostle Paul wrote, "I will not be brought under the power of any." What he means by that is, "I will not engage in anything that might get such a grip on me that I can't easily stop when I want." That, however, is the nature of gambling.

Reason #6: POOR STEWARDSHIP

Perhaps one of the most obvious problems with gambling is poor stewardship. In Matthew 25 we read the parable of the talents. We often use that parable to teach that we ought to use our talents in service to God, and that is not a misuse. But the word *talent* in this passage refers to a unit of money, just like we might use the term *dollar*. Some people think this is specifically a parable dealing with the stewardship of our money. Whether that is the specific point or not, it certainly has application. The point of that parable is that God expects us to be good stewards of the money (or whatever blessings) we possess. The man with one talent was not a good steward.

How does gambling relate to stewardship? Let's talk statistics for a moment. The odds of winning the lottery depend on where one plays. The odds can vary from 18 million to one all the way to 120 million to one. There is not a good chance either way. The odds of being struck by lightning are 2.65 million to one. On the high side, a person is 45 times more likely to die from a lightning strike than to win the lottery. They are 120 times more likely to die from flesh-eating bacteria than to win the lottery. The chances of an individual playing golf with three friends and two of them getting a hole-in-one in the same hole are better than winning the lottery. A person is 1,200 times more likely to die from a snake bite or bee sting than to win the lottery. If you drive 10 miles to purchase a lottery ticket, you are 20 times more likely to be killed in a car accident along the way than to win the jackpot.[4]

Two of the biggest lottery problems are Powerball and Mega Millions. For Powerball, the odds of winning the jackpot with any given ticket are one in 146,107,962. For Mega Millions, the odds are one in 175,711,536.[5] The odds of winning either of these are essentially zero. What if your financial

Odds of Winning
Powerball
1 in 146,107,962
Mega Millions
1 in 175,711,536

manager was sinking a certain portion of your retirement funds into a fund that had a one in 175 million—a virtual zero chance of being successful? How long would it take for you to fire him?

The lottery is sinful because the Lord holds us accountable for our stewardship. One man described the lottery as a tax on people who won't do the math. By that he meant that only people who don't understand the odds play the lottery.

Reason #7: THE INFLUENCE PRINCIPLE

Christians need to get a grip on this one. Even worldly people view gambling as a vice. It is an "adult activity." In South Carolina, the law states that a person must be 18 years of age to purchase a lottery ticket. Everyone has seen the commercials, "What goes on in Vegas, stays in Vegas." They show gambling, alcohol, and other sinful activities. There is a reason Las Vegas is called Sin City, and gambling is a big part of it.

A Christian who plays the lottery is devastating his influence. In 1 Corinthians 8:13 Paul wrote, "If food makes my brother stumble, I will never again eat meat, lest I make my brother stumble." Paul was so concerned about his influence that he said he would never again do something if it caused a problem, even something lawful, much less anything that violates Christian principles (such as gambling). James 1:27 says that pure, undefiled religion includes keeping yourself unspotted from the world. An old proverb goes like this: "In a bet there is a fool and a thief." Neither would do well for one's reputation.

OBJECTIONS MADE IN DEFENSE OF GAMBLING

Certainly, we all know that despite all of the problems with gambling, there are still folks who will make arguments in defense of it. One of those arguments is, "There's not a verse in the Bible that says *not* to." We have already mentioned this.

There is not a verse that specifically says, "Thou shalt not play Blackjack," but there are many verses that condemn it in principle, and Proverbs 13:11 does mention it.

Another argument made is, "Well, all of life is a risk!" But again, gambling is not wrong because of the risk. Someone might bet on something that is a surefire win, but it's still sinful.

Thirdly, some would say, "Gambling is really no different than investing in the stock market." But that's not true because the stock market is not an artificial risk. You profit or lose based on the economic performance of a company. In the stock market, you don't seek to gain at the direct loss of others. In economic gain, all profit is made by the exchange of goods and services. In the stock market, legitimate exchanges take place. Your money goes to work. Profiting from letting someone else use your money is not a sin, but an honest, economic principle (Matthew 25:14-30).

Fourthly, sometimes people will argue, "Good comes from it." This is the lie that so many states have been told by politicians when trying to legalize gambling. Lies like "We'll use it for education" and "It's good for the economy" are favorites of the devil. He uses them in many areas of life. Abortion is justified because of stem cell research to save lives. Alcohol is justified because of the health benefits (good for the heart). Gambling is justified because it's good for the economy.

GAMBLING

Michael Fitzgerald, a columnist for *The Record* (Stockton, California) disputes the economic argument for gambling, specifically in reference to casinos.

> He cites a 1994 study out of the University of Illinois that indicated the social problems created by gambling—addiction, domestic abuse, suicide, crime, indebtedness—outweigh by far any benefits to the community. In fact, the gambling enterprise costs "taxpayers three dollars for every one dollar of state revenue collected." Additionally, a Creighton University study found that "counties with casinos soon have double the bankruptcy rates of counties without casinos."[3]

Don't buy this "benefit" argument. According to information on the Nevada Resort Association website in January 2009, "over a third of all funding for Nevada's public schools comes from the gambling industry."[6] But when you consult the Nevada Department of Education, you find a different story. Their Quick Facts guide says that only 15 percent of educational funding comes from  gambling. The benefit argument is just another carefully crafted lie of the devil. Regardless, the Bible teaches that it is never right to do wrong. When Christians start reasoning that we will do wrong so that good may come, we have gotten ourselves into big trouble.

A fifth attempt to defend gambling says, "Well, I only spend a dollar a week. I only buy one lottery ticket per week. I'm not wasting much money. It's just a cheap way to have some fun. It gives me something to hope for." If you want something to hope for, lay up for yourselves treasures in heaven (Matthew 6:20). Regardless of what you say, you are wasting money. One dollar per week equals 52 dollars per year. For a missionary in Africa, 52 dollars could make a huge impact on the Lord's work. Certainly by gambling one hurts his influence. It's going to be hard to turn around and talk to the person behind you about the gospel when standing in line to buy a lottery ticket.

Some make this argument: "I only do a little." What if we apply that to other areas? A man looks at a little pornography. Someone uses the Lord's name in vain only a little. A woman cheats on her taxes a little. We must remember that a little wrong is still wrong.

Let's answer some questions. First, "What about sweepstakes, or door prizes, or a company giving away something in a drawing?" Is it wrong to enter your name in Publisher's Clearing House Sweepstakes? No. It doesn't fit the definition of gambling. Remember the three basic elements of gambling. In the sweepstakes there is no wager, it costs nothing, and the winner does not win at the direct loss of the others. In this situation, the prize is really a gift.

Then there's the question, "What about a cake raffle where you buy tickets?" That is gambling and a Christian should not participate in it.

CONCLUSION

The devil will tell us a lot of lies. He will tell us that it helps the schools, it's good for education, and it boosts the economy. But anything that takes from the poor, wreaks havoc on communities, promotes covetousness and addiction, and hurts one's reputation as a Christian is something of which we should want no part. Gambling is a sin, any way you roll the dice!

Video Resources

THE TRUTH ABOUT... GAMBLING

This video covers the continuing issue of gambling. Can Christians engage in methods of gambling? Should Christians be concerned with both sides, winning and losing?

TheTruthAbout.net/video/Gambling

DRINKING

A popular liquor commercial on television concludes with the words, "Drink responsibly." Alcohol commercials depict healthy, athletic people having a good time and engaging in outdoor adventures. Are these commercials accurate? Are they painting the true picture of what alcohol will do for you? Is it possible to drink responsibly?

Abraham Lincoln once said, "Alcohol has many defenders, but no defense."

THE EVIL EFFECTS OF ALCOHOL

Let's begin our study of alcohol with the words of Proverbs 20:1, "Wine is a mocker, strong drink is a brawler, and whoever is led astray by it is not wise."

In the United States of America, 700,000 people receive treatment for alcoholism every day.[1] In the year 2002, according to the National Highway Traffic Safety Administration, 41 percent of all the deaths that occurred in traffic accidents were alcohol-related.[2] That means that every 30 minutes, someone was killed in a traffic accident because of alcohol. If there were a disease that was killing off as many people, the government would be vehemently warning against it. Millions of dollars would be given to fund studies seeking a cure. There would be telethons to raise money to find a vaccine. Instead, alcohol is promoted and advertised at every turn. In the year 2000, the alcohol industry spent 1.42 billion dollars on television, radio, print, and outdoor advertising.[3] The resources spent on advertising alcohol are enough to feed 20 million people. One study says that young people view approximately 20,000 commercials each year, of which 2,000 are for beer and wine.[4] That is an average of more than five TV commercials per day.

1.42 BILLION DOLLARS
spent on televison, radio, print, and other advertising each year.

20 MILLION PEOPLE
could be fed with the advertising resources that are spent.

The median age at which people begin drinking is 15.7 years.[5] One statistic said college students spend approximately 5.5 billion dollars each year on alcohol. That's more than they spend on soft drinks, milk, juice, tea, coffee, and books combined.[6]

According to the National Institute on Alcohol Abuse and Alcoholism (NIAAA), one in every 13 adults—nearly 14 million Americans—abuse alcohol or are alcoholics.[7] Alcohol is involved in 50 percent of spousal abuse cases, 38 percent of child abuse cases, 65 percent of drownings, and 54 percent of imprisonments for violent crimes. Forty-nine percent of those convicted for murder, or attempted murder, had been under the influence of alcohol when they committed those crimes.[8] The list goes on and on with similar statistics.

ALCOHOL IS INVOLVED IN
50% of spousal abuse cases
38% of child abuse cases
65% of drownings
54% of imprisonments for violent crimes
49% of murders or attempted murders

Galatians 5:21 says that drunkenness is a "work of the flesh" committed by those who will not inherit the kingdom of God. The Bible is very pointed with regard to this subject. Amongst religious people, the controversy surrounding drinking is generally not over drunkenness; it's over what we call "social drinking" or "drinking in moderation." Social drinking would include drinking alcohol with one's meal, at weddings and parties, or in moderation with one's friends. For many people, the argument over alcohol begins at this point. This study will examine some of the arguments made by religious people and examine their best efforts to defend "social drinking."

DRINKING

ARGUMENTS MADE IN DEFENSE OF SOCIAL DRINKING

#1: There is no verse in the New Testament that specifically forbids drinking in moderation. All the verses address only the subject of drunkenness.

There are many things that are not specifically condemned in the Scriptures that are still wrong. Using heroin is not specifically condemned, but who is going to argue that since the New Testament does not specifically command people to abstain from heroin, its use is permissible? Many activities are forbidden based upon biblical principles. It is important to observe, however, that drinking alcohol is specifically forbidden and forbidden in principle. Someone might ask, "Where does the Bible specifically forbid drinking?" The answer is, "In every verse where it forbids drunkenness."

At first glance this may not be readily apparent, so let's illustrate this point. In Ephesians 5:18, the King James Version says, "And be not drunk with wine, wherein is excess; but be filled with the Spirit." The phrase, "be not drunk," is translated from the Greek root *methusko*. This word means: 1) "to begin to be softened," Young's Analytical Concordance; 2) "to moisten, or to be moistened with liquor, and in a figurative sense, to be saturated with drink," S. T. Bloomfield; 3) "to grow drunk" (marking the beginning of *methuo*), E. W. Bullinger. *Methusko* is an inceptive verb.[9] It is a word that marks the process of becoming drunk. What Paul is actually saying in Ephesians 5 is, "Do not begin the process of becoming drunk."

When a person consumes alcohol, he is beginning to be softened and intoxicated. That's why social drinking is condemned in the words *drunk* or *drunkenness*. The implication is that people begin to be drunk when they begin to drink. The reason people struggle with this is probably because of what they don't see. If they don't see the person staggering around or in

> People begin to be drunk when they begin to drink.
>
> **EPHESIANS 5:18**
> "And be not drunk with wine..."

a drunken stupor, they don't consider him to be drunk. But that is not the basis upon which the Bible determines drunkenness.

Science and medical studies also bear out the fact that when a person begins to drink, he is drunk to some degree. How much alcohol does a person have to consume in order to be affected? As early as the 1960s, the *Journal of the American Medical Association* stated, "There is no minimum (blood-alcohol concentration or BAC) which can be set, at which there will be absolutely no effect."[9]

Someone might protest, "Well, that's old. We're wiser now. We've had scientific advancements in the last 40 years." Consider this quote from the *Journal of the American Medical Association*, May 3, 2000: "Although legal limits for BAC levels have been set in most states, impairment in driving skills can occur with any amount of alcohol in the bloodstream."[10]

A website overseen by the University of Oklahoma Police Department allows a person to enter his weight, what he is drinking, the length of time, and the number of drinks. Using that information, the website calculates one's approximate

BAC (blood alcohol content). For example, a 160-pound man with one drink (five ounces) of fortified dessert wine (drinking it immediately) puts him at 0.05 percent blood alcohol content. A 160-pound man with one drink (12 ounces) of reduced alcohol beer (over a one-hour period) puts him at 0.02 percent BAC. Another website says that at 0.02 percent BAC there is loss of judgment, relaxation, slight body warmth, altered mood, decline in visual functions (rapid track of moving target), and decline in ability to perform two tasks at the same time (divided attention).

The world admits some amount of drunkenness—impairment, loss of judgment, and soberness—with one drink. In light of that, how can a Christian possibly defend social drinking? With one drink, a person is already affected, or impaired to that extent, and it gets worse with each consecutive drink. The Bible does condemn social drinking. It's in the verses that discuss drunkenness.

First Peter 4:3 states, "For we have spent enough of our past lifetime in doing the will of the Gentiles–when we walked in lewdness, lusts, drunkenness, revelries, drinking parties, and abominable idolatries." Notice that Peter condemns drinking parties.

The famous commentator, Albert Barnes, wrote about this verse: "The idea in the passage is that it is improper for Christians to meet together for the purpose of drinking." This decisively condemns "social drinking."

The reference book, *Synonyms of the New Testament*, by Richard Trench, states that this Greek word means "the drinking bout, the banquet, the symposium not of necessity excessive... but giving opportunity for excess." If this is the correct understanding of this word, then the idea is that drinking parties are wrong regardless of whether or not one becomes drunk.

Albert Barnes commented on the phrase drinking parties, "The thing forbidden by it is an assembling together for the purpose of drinking ... The idea in the passage is, that it is improper for Christians to meet together for the purpose of drinking—as wine, toasts, etc. ... It would forbid, therefore, an attendance on all those celebrations in which drinking toasts is understood to be an essential part of the  festivities, and all those where hilarity and joyfulness are sought to be produced by the intoxicating bowl. Such are not proper places for Christians."

#2: Ephesians 5:18 shows that alcohol is only wrong when used in excess, thus moderate drinking is okay.

Ephesians 5:18 says, "And be not drunk with wine, wherein is excess; but be filled with the Spirit." The defender of drinking argues, "Drinking alcohol in moderation is not condemned. It is only drinking in excess that is sinful."

This argument is really a misunderstanding of the word *excess*. That word does not refer to an excessive amount of alcohol; it refers to excessive (ungodly) behavior. The American Standard Version reads, "And be not drunk with wine, wherein is riot." This better conveys the meaning of the passage. The idea then (remembering this is an inceptive verb) is, "Do not begin drinking alcohol which brings ungodly behavior, but rather be filled with the Spirit, which will have the opposite effect."

#3: Drinking wine has health benefits.

One of the arguments made by those seeking to defend social drinking is that it is actually beneficial to one's health. They sometimes cite the results of a study which states that drinking one glass of wine per day is good.

First, this argument diverts attention from the real issue. When people gather together to drink socially, they  are not doing it for the health benefits. When people host a party with an open bar, they are serving alcohol out of concern for people's hearts and medical conditions. This argument is a smokescreen.

The study often cited states that there is a chemical substance in wine called resveratrol, which helps prevent cardiovascular disease and cancer. An excerpt from the Mayo Clinic website, dated March 9, 2007 states:

> *The American Heart Association doesn't recommend that you start drinking alcohol just to prevent heart disease. Alcohol can be addictive. Too much increases your risk of high blood pressure, high triglycerides, liver damage, obesity, certain types of cancer, accidents, and other problems. In addition, even small amounts of alcohol can cause cardiomyopathy—weakened heart muscle—and heart failure in some people.*[11]

Martha Grogan, cardiologist from the Mayo Clinic received the question, "Does grape juice have the same health benefits as red wine?" She answered:

> There is evidence that drinking red wine may reduce your risk of heart disease. This benefit is most likely due to a substance called resveratrol found in the skin and seeds of grapes–especially dark red and purple grapes. Resveratrol is also found in grape juice—especially juice made from the dark purple Concord grapes. Recent studies have suggested that red and purple grape juice may provide the same heart-healthy benefits of red wine.[12]

She goes on to say, "Both red wine and grape juice also contain antioxidants... which have been shown to increase your... good... cholesterol and lower your risk of clogged arteries... and may help lower blood pressure."

#4: Paul told Timothy to drink wine for the sake of his stomach.

In 1 Timothy 5:23 Paul writes, "No longer drink only water, but use a little wine for your stomach's sake and your frequent infirmities." This passage is not discussing having alcohol at a party or with friends. It is discussing using alcohol as a medicine, like Nyquil.

Most people believe Timothy's stomach problem was related to the water in Asia Minor, which could be very dangerous. Paul's statement is elliptical and means, "Be no longer a drinker of water [alone], but [with it] take a little wine."

There is a big difference between Nyquil and Budweiser.

1 TIMOTHY 5:23 does not support having a beer with buddies.

It is also worth noticing that Paul had to instruct Timothy to drink wine for his stomach's sake, which suggests two things. First, Timothy had reservations about doing it. Second, if it was common for the early Christians to do this, then Paul's encouragement would not have been needed here.

On a side note, there is a significant difference between Nyquil and Budweiser. The person who wants to defend having a beer with his buddies is not going to find support for it in 1 Timothy 5:23.

#5: In Bible times they had no way to prevent fermentation, therefore they must have drunk alcoholic wine.

Let's briefly discuss the fermentation process. Grape juice is composed of two leading elements, sugar and gluten. The decay of the gluten causes the growth of yeast germs. In the presence of the yeast, the sugar in grape juice is gradually converted into alcohol. The ancients had actually figured out a number of different ways to prevent this process from occurring. W. D. Jeffcoat in his book, *The Bible and Social Drinking*, goes into a detailed explanation of the four processes used to keep fermentation from happening.[9]

First is boiling: The water evaporates and fermentation cannot occur. Water is added again later to reconstitute the juice.

Second is sulfur: The juice is exposed to sulfur flames, then sealed and kept cool until used.

> **WAYS TO PREVENT FERMENTATION**
> 1. Boiling
> 2. Sulfur
> 3. Cooling
> 4. Filtration

Third is cooling: The juice is placed in airtight jars and immersed in springs or stored in caves where the temperature remains below 45 degrees Fahrenheit.

The fourth is filtration: The yeast is strained out of the juice, thereby stopping the fermentation process.

Plutarch said, "Wine is rendered old or feeble when it is frequently filtered. The strength of the spirit being thus excluded, the wine neither inflames the brain nor infests the mind and passions, and is much more pleasant to drink."

#6: Jesus turned water into wine at the wedding feast in Cana of Galilee.

It is not always the case that any time we see the word wine in the Bible it refers to an alcoholic drink. Wine is a generic word. It can refer to either fermented or unfermented juice of the grape. The context must determine which type is meant.

Alcoholic wine is mentioned in Proverbs 23:31-32, "Do not look on the wine when it is red, when it sparkles in the cup, when it swirls around smoothly; at the last it bites like a serpent, and stings like a viper."

Non-alcoholic wine is talked about in Isaiah 16:10, "In the vineyards there will be no singing, nor will there be shouting; no treaders will tread out wine in the presses." Isaiah 65:8 says, "As the new wine is found in the cluster, and one says, 'Do not destroy it, for a blessing is in it,' so will I do for my servants' sake, that I may not destroy them all." The wine is mentioned as being still in the grapes, but it is called wine. In all of these passages the same Hebrew word is translated by our English word *wine*.

The same principle is true in the New Testament. There are five different Greek terms for wine. The one most commonly used is *oinos*. It is used of both fermented wine and unfermented wine (grape juice). When reading the Scriptures, one should never assume that word *wine* always refers to alcoholic wine.

The person making the argument that Jesus endorsed social drinking by turning water into wine at Cana has to prove that it was alcoholic wine. That is difficult because the context indicates just the opposite. Notice in John 2:10 that after Jesus had turned the water into wine, the governor of the feast tasted it, and said, "Every man at the beginning sets out the good wine, and when the guests have well drunk, then the inferior. You have kept the good wine until now!"

DRINKING

The interesting phrase in this verse is "well drunk." Some translations translate is as "drunk freely." Thomas Summers states "drunk freely" suggests the idea of largely drinking. The way we might say this today is, "They drank until they had plenty." If this were truly alcoholic wine, then these people would have already violated the passages that everyone would agree prohibit drunkenness. If alcoholic wine is under

consideration, then it describes a group of people who had "drunk freely" of alcoholic wine. They had drunk alcoholic wine until they were "well wined." They had drunk alcoholic wine until they "had plenty," and then Jesus made 120-160 gallons more of alcoholic wine for people who had already finished off the first round. How could the Lord forbid

drunkenness and then do that? It is also interesting to note that the governor of the feast had not had his senses dulled. He could readily discern the "good" wine from the "worse" which is indicative of the fact that he had not been drinking alcoholic wine.

The point is *oinos* (wine) can refer either to an alcoholic or non-alcoholic drink, and the context of John 2 points to non-alcoholic wine.

#7: 1 Timothy 3:3 says elders are required to "Not be given to wine," whereas in verse 8 deacons are to "Not be given to <u>much</u> wine."

This position argues that elders can't have any wine, but deacons can drink in moderation. The basis of their dispute is the phrase "not given to wine" with reference to elders and "not be given to much wine" with reference to deacons. These phrases supposedly give implied consent to deacons to drink in small quantities.

First, we need to understand that a warning against excess can never be used as approval for the action itself. For example, the Ephesians 4:26 says, "Let not the sun go down on your wrath." This verse is not an approval for practicing wrath prior to sundown. A warning against one activity is not implied consent for another.

First Peter 4:3-4 again shows the fallacy of the "implied consent" argument. Verse 3 mentions the "excess of wine." Those looking to justify the use of alcoholic beverages might look at this and say, "See, this verse only condemns wine in excess." Or they might argue that this verse implies consent for wine, so long as it isn't excessive. In other words, moderate drinking is not sinful. Observe, however, that the passage goes on in the next verse to discuss the "excess of riot." If this "implied consent" argument is accurate, then we also have divine sanction for riot in moderation. And what about Ecclesiastes 7:17 which says, "Be not overmuch wicked"? (ASV). Would that imply that we have the right to be a little wicked? James 1:21 says, "Therefore lay aside all filthiness and overflow of wickedness." Would this mean it would be alright to have wickedness as long as it isn't overflowing? Of course not.

Appreciate the level of absurdity to which the implied consent argument will take a person. Let's assume for a moment that the argument that elders can't drink but deacons can is true. The same phrase that is applied to deacons in 1 Timothy 3:8 is applied to the aged women in Titus 2:3. So the aged women could also drink in moderation. But interestingly enough it is not applied to the younger women. Therefore the younger women could not drink. In addition, 1 Timothy 3:11, in describing deacons' wives uses the word "sober" (KJV). The New King James uses the word "temperate." The Greek word *nephaleous* means to abstain from wine. Titus 2:2 requires aged men not to come near wine (*me parionon*).

Let's put it all together. Elders cannot drink, but deacons can. Older men cannot drink, but older women can. Deacons can drink, but their wives cannot. Who can believe this? It is absolute nonsense! This, however, is where these arguments in defense of social drinking will take a person.[13]

#8: In Luke 7:33-34 Jesus was accused of being a "winebibber." This accusation would not have been made had He not been drinking alcoholic wine.

Luke 7:33-34 says, "For John the Baptist came neither eating bread nor drinking wine, and you say, 'He has a demon.' The Son of Man has come eating and drinking, and you say, 'Look, a glutton and a winebibber, a friend of tax collectors and sinners!'"

The argument is that the people would not have accused Jesus of being a winebibber or a drunkard if he had not been drinking alcoholic wine. It should be observed, however, that the people also said John had a demon. Where was the evidence for that? There was none. That was a lie and so was the accusation of Jesus being a drinker. The people were jumping to conclusions not warranted by evidence. There is no argument here.

#9: Colossians 2:16 says, "So let no one judge you in food or in drink, or regarding a festival or a new moon or sabbaths..."

It is argued that we have no right to judge another person with regard to what they eat or drink. In truth, this passage is dealing with matters of liberty or matters of opinion, not with matters in which the Lord has mandated right or wrong. These were issues relating to the Old Law. Some were trying to bind the food and drink issue of the Law of Moses. The point of Colossians 2:16 is, "Don't let any man bind on you what God has not." The Old Law has been nailed to the cross. We are not accountable to it. The liberty discussed in this passage related to food and drink which was considered ceremonially clean or unclean during the Mosaic period. It has nothing to do with matters that are sinful today, such as drinking alcohol.

CONCLUSION

If you are not convinced that the Bible prohibits drinking, there is still one more factor to consider, and that is your influence. When a person who professes to be a Christian drinks alcoholic beverages, he is doing something that even the world sees as an adult vice, and it greatly damages his influence. Also, he is likely to become

a stumbling block to young Christians and new converts.

In 1 Corinthians 8:10-13 Paul discusses meat offered to idols. The context is different from our present discussion because he is referencing an activity not wrong in and of itself. Those who defend social drinking mistakenly believe it not to be sinful either. But listen to Paul: "For if anyone sees you who have knowledge eating in an idol's temple, will not the conscience of him who is weak be emboldened to eat those things offered to idols? And because of your knowledge shall the weak brother perish, for whom Christ died? But when you thus sin against the brethren, and wound their weak conscience, you sin against Christ. Therefore, if food makes my brother stumble, I will never again eat meat, lest I make my brother stumble." Paul is saying, "Someone may see me doing it, and it may cause him to sin, and in light of that, I will never do it."

Matthew 5:16 says, "Let your light so shine before men, that they may see your good works and glorify your Father in heaven." It will be a lot harder for a person to do that with a beer in his hand. In fact, it will be impossible.

Wilson Thomas lived in Bradenton, Florida. On one particular day, Mr. Thomas had had a hard day at work and stopped by the local bar to have a few drinks and unwind before he went home to his son, Randall. Wilson paid for his drinks and took an additional bottle with him. When he was almost home a young boy on a bicycle darted out in front of him. He swerved to miss him and perhaps would have, had his senses not been dulled by alcohol. The boy was dead. In a panic Mr. Thomas fled the scene and rushed home. Several hours later, when the police came to arrest him, they found him in his attic, drinking and crying. It was only then that he realized the boy he'd hit was his own son Randall.

"Wine is a mocker, strong drink is a brawler, and whoever is led astray by it is not wise" (Proverbs 20:1).

Video Resources

THE TRUTH ABOUT... DRINKING

This video covers the controversial topic of Social Drinking. Can Christians engage in social drinking? What constitutes drunkenness?

TheTruthAbout.net/video/Drinking

Dancing

It is amazing how many songs have the word *dance* in them. Michael Buble sings, "Save the Last Dance for Me." Lady Gaga sings "Just Dance." Whitney Houston sang, "I Wanna Dance with Somebody."

Recently on television dancing has become the latest prime time rage. Fox has "So You Think You Can Dance." ABC has "Dancing with the Stars" which is boasting 22.5 million viewers on Monday nights.[1] Dancing is extremely popular and an obstacle with which young people are regularly faced. There are the school dances, most notably the prom, prompting kids have to ask, "Should I go?" It's a tough issue. For a teen to say, "No, I'm not going to the prom" or "I'm not going to the dance" makes him or her seem out of touch, maybe old fashioned, and will likely bring ridicule from peers.

Dancing is obviously a timely, relevant topic, and one that we need to consider to see what the Bible has to say on the subject. One's reaction will reveal a lot about his attitude toward divine guidelines.

Take a moment and ask yourself, "Am I one who seeks to avoid questionable activities," or "Do I try to walk as close to sin as possible and sacrifice as little as I can for the Lord?" Your answers to these questions are relevant as we discuss dancing.

Dancing
"To move rhythmically usually to music, using prescribed or improvised steps and gestures."

Let's begin our study by defining our terms. Dictionary.com defines dancing as follows: "To move rhythmically usually to music, using prescribed or improvised steps and gestures."

The word dance (including danced, dances, and dancing) is used 27 times in the Bible. There are six Old Testament (Hebrew) words translated as *dance*. There are two New Testament (Greek) words translated as *dance*. When one reads those 27 occurrences, he will find that these words are used in two different ways. The first is "to jump up and down with joy," as an enthusiastic fan does when his team scores. This is a celebratory action. In 1 Samuel 6:14-16 when the Ark of the Covenant was finally returned to Jerusalem, David danced. In Exodus 15 Miriam led the women in dance and song, praising God for bringing them safely through the Red Sea. When *dance* is used in this sense it is a synonym for happiness or celebration.

Dancing In The Bible
(usage #1)
"To jump up and down with joy"
(A synonym for happiness or celebration)
(usage #2)
"Men and women interacting together like they would at a party"

The second sense in which *dance* is used is in the sense of men and women interacting as they would at a party, dance club, or prom. In Exodus 32 while Moses was on the mountain receiving the Ten Commandments, the children of Israel made a golden calf. They danced around it and engaged in immoral conduct, and Moses strongly condemned them for it. Every time men danced with women in the Old and New Testaments, the act was condemned.

It is this second type of dancing that we are considering in this study--the kind that would take place at a night club or a high school dance. What does the Bible say about this type of dancing? Someone might respond, "Nothing! There is no passage in the Bible that says, 'Thou shalt not dance.'" It is true that this particular quotation does not appear in the Bible, however, there are passages and principles that address dancing.

WHY DANCING IS WRONG

#1: Galatians 5:19

In Galatians 5:19 Paul begins listing the works of the flesh, "Now the works of the flesh are manifest, which are these; adultery, fornication, uncleanness, lasciviousness ... "

Dancing

Notice *lasciviousness*. We don't use this word much anymore. Most mothers probably don't warn their children before they go on a date, "Drive carefully, and don't engage in lasciviousness!" The New King James Version uses "lewdness" instead. Other versions use terms such as "sensuality" and "lustful pleasure." According to Thayer's Greek Lexicon, the Greek word here means, "wanton manners as filthy words, indecent bodily movements, unchaste handling of males and females."

Lasciviousness
"Wanton manners as filthy words, indecent bodily movements, unchaste handling of males and females."

Reread this defintion and try to envision what one would have to do to be guilty of this. What involves indecent bodily movements? What involves unchaste handling of males and females? It's dancing! If dancing does not fit this description, what does? Dances are typically held in dimly lit environments. Dresses are usually low-cut. The dance itself involves males and females holding each other closely and rubbing their bodies together to the rhythm of suggestive music. *Dancing with the Stars* is not a show that a Christian should watch, but if you have ever seen even a commercial for it, it perfectly depicts lasciviousness. The Greek word translated *lasciviousness* is found nine times in the New Testament. Six times it is translated as "lasciviousness," two times as "wantonness," and one time as "filthy." In modern language we would define it as "conduct which excites lust."

In Galatians 5:21 Paul writes, "They which do such things shall not inherit the kingdom of God." To put it plainly, those who engage in this type of dancing are not going to heaven.

Another activity that fits our definition, and is really a type of dancing, is cheerleading. It is not a sin to cheer for a team, and cheerleading is not inherently sinful. Most of the time, however, cheerleading involves young women in short skirts that fly

up during their routines. They are engaging in very provocative movements, sometimes sexual in nature. These days, it's in vogue to have male and female cheerleaders, such that boys are holding and tossing the girls and intimately handling their bodies.

Again, there is nothing wrong with showing team spirit, but when cheerleading involves provocative gyrations and immodest movements such as the norm today, it fits the definition of that which the Lord said will keep a person out of heaven.

Someone may argue, "You're crazy! It's not like that!" But there is a reason cheerleaders wear skimpy outfits even in the dead of winter, and it's more than just team spirit.

#2: Matthew 5:28

Jesus said, "But I say to you that whoever looks at a women to lust for her has already committed adultery with her in his heart" (Matthew 5:28). The Lord taught us that when a male lusts for a female to whom he is not married, he is doing something inherently sinful. This is the problem with dancing. It is strongly sexual in nature and arouses lust. Sandra Humphrey, author of *Don't Kiss Toads*, wrote, "No healthy man will deny that it is sexually arousing to watch a girl swing her hips and breasts suggestively to music."[2]

The Bible provides a real-life illustration of the sexual effects of dancing. You are probably familiar with the story of Herod and Herodias. Mark 6:21-22 says, "Then an opportune day came when Herod on his birthday gave a feast for his nobles, the high officers, and the chief men of Galilee. And when Herodias' daughter herself came in and danced, and pleased Herod and those who sat with him, the king said to the girl, 'Ask me whatever you want, and I will give it to you.'"

Notice that the text says she danced before them. She engaged in suggestive movements while they watched. What was Herod's reaction? The passage says that it "pleased" him. The Greek word is *aresko*, and it carries the idea of exciting

emotion. We are being told that Herod was sexually pleased (stimulated) by her dancing. The result was that he made a foolish vow he soon regretted. His rashness is an example of how this type of dancing (this type of arousal) causes a man to do things that he might not normally do.

Consider this, too. What if Herod had danced with her? Would that have made it any better? If he had handled her as men handle women in a modern dance, would that have made it less evil? Of course not. In fact, it would have been worse. Paul Southern wrote that dancing "is like building a fire under a tea kettle and daring the water to boil."[3] Dancing arouses sexual passions and lust.

Someone might say, "I just don't buy into the idea of dancing being sexual. It's just fun. There's nothing sexual to it." If that is true then why don't we have a father/son dance? There are father/son ballgames and father/son camp outs. But you've never seen a father/son dance. If there is nothing sexual about dancing, why don't school officials let the boys dance in the cafeteria while the girls dance in the gym? We all know that would be the end of the party. The world understands the sexual nature of dancing. Mick Jagger, lead singer for the Rolling Stones, said, "All dancing is replacement for sex." Dr. Leta S. Hollingworth said, "Dancing is an exciting and pleasurable recreation, as it affords a partial satisfaction of the sex impulse. Dancing, in fact, is such an erotic stimuli that it even works for boys and girls as young as age 11."[4]

Mick Jagger

"All dancing is a replacement for sex."

In one study, 44 boys were asked what their feelings were toward young ladies with whom they danced. Forty-one of them (93 percent) said they thought about sex. An audience of 1,500 men was asked, "How many can dance and not have evil thoughts?" No hands were raised. In another study, 80 percent of men admitted to having lustful thoughts while dancing.[3] The point is, dancing stimulates sexual thoughts and feelings and violates what Jesus said in Matthew 5:28.

Dancing

#3: Dancing is a prelude to other sins.

When a male and a female come together and begin to handle each other, shake their bodies in front of each other while moving to music, hold each other tightly (pressed against one another), sexual tension builds. The participants are begging for trouble and flirting with temptation.

The writer of Proverbs tells his son about the immoral woman in Proverbs 5, "Remove your way far from her, and do not go near the door of her house." The idea is, "Get away. Stay away. Don't see how close you can get to temptation." First Corinthians 6:18 says, "Flee fornication." We are not to be enticed by it. First Peter 2:11 says to "abstain from fleshly lusts which war against the soul."

Orphanages say that nine months after school proms they have extra babies to care for. Why? Because dancing is a prelude to other sins. The Roman Catholic Confessional reveals that of their girls who go wrong, 19 of every 20 attribute their sin to dancing.[3] With reference to school dances, sometimes people will say, "How can something be wrong when it is so tightly supervised? Nothing's going to happen."

First, that simply isn't true. It's impossible to watch everyone every second. "Things do happen." Second, chaperones can control only what happens outwardly. They cannot control thoughts. They cannot control lusts that build up inside those young boys. They certainly cannot control what takes place on the way home or at any time after the dance. Furthermore, the fact that the prom and other school dances have to be so tightly chaperoned in the first place ought to tell us something.

Somebody phrased it this way, "When you turn a guy on, he can be awfully hard to turn off." A *Reader's Digest* survey from 1999 said that over 75 percent of young women and 65 percent of young men who had not yet had intimate sexual relations planned to change that on prom night.[5] Consider also some of the more popular prom dresses. Not trying

1999 Reader's Digest Survey
Over 75% of young women and 65% of young men who had not yet had sexual relations planned to change that on prom night.

to be crude, but some them look like the attire of a prostitute. The ads for prom dresses sum it up well. Cybergown.com on their page for "Prom Fashion 2009" says, "The sexy necklines... look good, but try not to wear a necklace for a more astonishing sexy look.... This time the prom dresses have become more and more alluring and seductive."[6] Promgirl.net recommends workouts to get girls in shape for the prom. The accompanying article reads, "Performing these prom workouts and exercises can assure a phenomenal body just in time for the event of the season. With time and effort, you will undoubtedly turn some heads with your terrific toned look!"[7] *Sexy, alluring,* and *seductive* are not the goals of young ladies trying to please God.

#4: 1 Corinthians 15:33

First Corinthians 15:33 says, "Be not deceived: evil companionships corrupt good morals."

Use your imagination for a moment and think about the kind of people who participate in modern dance. Who would frequent a dance club? Men and women go there to engage in things that are enticing and titillating.

Think about the companions of dance itself. What does one usually find at dances? Alcohol; very revealing, sexually provocative clothing; and often, suggestive, crude, and crass music.

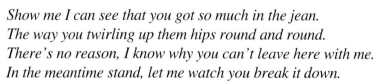

As an example, we have listed a few of the top 10 prom dance songs for 2009. Number 1 was "Just Dance" by Lady Gaga.[8] Consider the lyrics:

Show me I can see that you got so much in the jean.
The way you twirling up them hips round and round.
There's no reason, I know why you can't leave here with me.
In the meantime stand, let me watch you break it down.

The lyrics to this song are a great summary of the points we've been making about dancing.

Number three on the list was "I Kissed a Girl," a song about two females kissing each other. Number seven on the top 10 prom dance songs was "Sexyback" by Justin Timberlake.[8] Here is an excerpt of its lyrics:

Dirty babe (uh-huh).
You see the shackles. Baby, I'm your slave (uh-huh).
I'll let you whip me if I misbehave (uh-huh).
It's just that no one makes me feel this way (uh-huh).

These songs are listed as the top dance songs for the prom! These are for high school kids. Not that they would be appropriate for adults, but the fact that these are the songs that are being played for young people while they dance ought to alarm us.

Questions About Dancing

#1: What about dancing for exercise?

Sometimes people say, "I just like to dance because it's good exercise, not for any of those things you're discussing." If a person wants to dance alone in the privacy of his or her own home for exercise, that's fine. It is when other people become involved that the problems we've been discussing arise.

#2: What about dancing when it's just between a husband and wife in the privacy of their own home?

This is a common question asked by Christians, perhaps because of all of the teaching done stating that dancing is wrong. Dancing, however, is not inherently wrong. It is the sexual aspects, the immodesty and the environment that create problems. If a married couple wants to dance in the privacy of their home, more power to them. Certainly there is nothing wrong with that. It might even be good for their relationship.

 **Dancing**

WHAT ABOUT THINGS LIKE THE "HOKEY POKEY?"

Believe it or not, some people object to the Hokey Pokey and other such innocent games. It's doubtless that any of us have ever seen the Hokey Pokey performed in a way that fits the description of inappropriate dance. Christians have to use good sense with regard to questions like these. There is nothing wrong with doing the Hokey Pokey.

CONCLUSION

The story is told of a young girl who was part of a group scheduled to tour a coal mine. The girl arrived dressed in her spotless white dress. Her friends told her that she was ridiculous to wear a white dress into the coal mine. The girl responded, "Oh, it will be all right. I'll be careful not to touch anything dirty." She then turned to the miner who was leading the tour and asked, "Is there anything to prevent me from wearing a white dress into the coal mine?" He responded, "No, there's nothing to keep you from wearing a white dress in, but there are many things that will keep you from wearing a white dress out."

James 1:27 says that pure and undefiled religion involves keeping oneself unspotted from the world, but that is awfully hard to do when we surround ourselves with filth. Dancing is lascivious. It is sexual in nature and promotes lust. It is a prelude to other sinful activities, and it involves wicked companions. It is impossible for a Christian to keep himself or herself unspotted from the world while participating in the modern-day dance.

In Sherry Burgess's tract *Shall I Go To The Prom?* she writes, "One night was hard, God held my hand, He gave me courage to take a stand. It doesn't hurt me anymore, I'm stronger than I was before. One night was hard, I made a stand, and now there's left the Promised Land."

Video Resources

THE TRUTH ABOUT... DANCING

This video covers the topic of Modern Dancing. Can Christians participate in modern dancing? What are the moral implications involved?

TheTruthAbout.net/video/Dancing

"Have you ever told a lie?" Most all of us would probably have to answer "yes," at least once, likely many times. Lying is a subject that is almost universal in nature. And we have a tendency to classify lies. Some lies we think of as big lies, while we deem other lies as insignificant. Let's begin our discussion of lying by asking the question, "What does God really think about lying?"

Is being truthful a daily challenge? Certainly we face challenges in our lives, but not all challenges are daily ones. Some years ago there was a study indicating that the average person lies twenty-five times a day. Do you believe that could be accurate?

Think about the many situations in which people lie. Dad comes home after a long day at work, and as the family is sitting down to relax and eat dinner, the telephone rings. Another family member answers, and finds the call is for dad...and it's a telemarketer. It is so easy to say, "Tell them I'm not here!" Sometimes one might say it before he even stops to think about it. If you start adding up incidents like this, then yes, perhaps the average person *does* lie twenty-five times a day. Hopefully Christians do not, but the average person does.

According to one poll, the majority of people interviewed said they *have* lied and *would* do so again, either to protect

> Lying by the numbers
>
> The majority of people polled said they HAVE lied and WOULD lie again:
> 1) To protect themselves
> 2) To keep from hurting someone's feelings

themselves or to keep from hurting someone else's feelings. This author believes it would hurt him more to discover that he had been lied to! This poll tells us that most people do not have a problem with lying. Or maybe we should say most people **do** have a problem with lying!

People say they lie to protect themselves, to keep from hurting others, and also to get out of trouble. This last one seems to be a common reason to lie. One writer has defined a lie as "a coward's way of getting out of trouble." This is a fitting definition because sometimes it takes some real courage and moral fiber to tell the truth.

At what *age* does lying become a problem for people? This question was once asked of a group of people to which one responded, "As soon as they learn to talk." That seems quite accurate. It's likely one of the first sins that people commit. They get caught doing something wrong and lie to avoid getting in trouble. And it certainly doesn't stop with children. All of us can call to mind images of government officials lying and committing perjury to keep themselves out of trouble.

Sadly, lying is one of those sins that people tend to think of as not a big deal. We think, "Ah, what's it going to hurt?" With that thought in mind, let's consider Proverbs 6:16-19: "These six things the Lord hates, yes, seven are an abomination to Him: A proud look, *a lying tongue*, hands that shed innocent blood, a heart that devises wicked plans, feet that are swift in running to evil, *a false witness who speaks lies*, and one who sows discord among brethren." Notice that in this short list of seven things God hates, two of the things mentioned are "a lying tongue" and "a false witness that speaks lies." Two of the seven things God despises involve lying. On our human scale, lying doesn't rank high up there, but what about God's scale? On the Sin-O-Meter (if there were such a thing), God is saying, "Here are seven things I despise, that are an abomination, that are particularly repulsive in my sight, and lying is one of them." In fact, we might say that lying is two of them. With that being the case, if we are going to be right, we need to change our perspective on how we look at things. We need to start looking at lying the way God looks at it.

Let's define "lying." Webster's Dictionary defines lying, "to utter falsehood with an intention to deceive...to cause an incorrect impression; to present a misleading appearance..."

In light of this definition, do you think a person can lie without actually saying the words? Sometimes people will bend over backwards to lead someone to believe something that is not true, but they will not actually say the words. Afterwards they will say, "Well, I didn't lie." Sometimes in court people play this type of game. Sometimes lawyers will meet with their clients before they go to court to tutor them on how to give a false impression without perjuring themselves. Even though they may not state the lie outright, it is still a lie. Essentially, this means: you lie whenever you cause someone to believe something that is not true, and you do it intentionally. This, however, is not referring to a mistake or miscommunication; everyone makes mistakes. What's under discussion here is *intentionally* deceiving someone.

> Can a person lie without actually saying the words?

GOD AND LYING

First, let's consider God and lying. As we ponder the ethics of lying, appreciate that *God cannot lie*. It is impossible for Him to do it. Titus 1:2 says of the Christian's eternal life, "... God, that cannot lie, promised before the world began." What does that mean? It means that when God says something, we can absolutely count on it, because He will not and cannot lie. When God promises eternal life to the faithful, we can believe it is going to happen. 2 Peter 3:8 says, "...beloved, do not forget this one thing, that with the Lord one day is as a thousand years, and a thousand years as one day." In the context of 2 Peter 3 it was prophesied that in the latter days some people would deny that the Lord is going to return. Their reasoning was, "It's been thousands of years, and nothing has happened. It's not going to happen." But the text says "one day is as a thousand years, and a thousand years as one day." The point is that God's promises are true whether He made them yesterday or thousands of years ago. How can we know for sure? Because God cannot lie. Every promise in the Bible *will* come to pass. When God promises eternal life to the faithful, it will come to pass. When He promises eternal punishment to the wicked, it too will come to pass.

Occasionally, at the passing of a non-Christian friend, someone will suggest that God will save him despite the fact that he was not a Christian, but simply on the basis of the fact that he was a "good person." It is, however, impossible for that to happen, because God cannot lie, and 2 Thessalonians 1:8 says that on the Day of Judgment Christ will come in flaming fire "taking vengeance on those who do not know God, *and on those who do not obey the gospel of our Lord Jesus Christ.*" If a person has not obeyed the gospel, he will not be saved. If he is saved, then God is a liar, but our first point has already been established that God cannot lie.

Secondly, God hates lying. Not only can He *not* lie, He hates it. Proverbs 6:17 says lying is an abomination to the Lord. Proverbs 12:22 similarly says, "Lying lips are an abomination to the Lord; but they that deal truly are His delight." So it is clear how God feels about lying. He *despises* it.

Thirdly, lying is contrary to the nature of God. Now what is the nature of God? The Bible says that God is truth. When Christ walked upon this earth, He said, "I am the way, *the truth*, and the life; no man comes to the Father, but by me (John 14:6)." In addition, His word is truth. The Psalmist wrote, "For the word of the Lord is right; and all His works are done in truth" (Psalm 33:4). John wrote, "Sanctify them through Thy truth; Thy word is truth" (John 17:17). Psalm 31:5 calls God the "God of truth."

God and Lying
1. God cannot lie
2. God hates lying
3. Lying is contrary to God's nature

God cannot lie; He hates lying; it is contrary to His nature; and God forbids His children to lie. The Old Law said, "You shall not steal, *nor deal falsely, nor lie to one another*" (Leviticus 19:11). The Ten Commandments stated, "You shall not bear false witness against your neighbor" (Exodus 20:16). In the New Testament, included in the list with the cowardly, unbelieving, abominable, murderers, sexually immoral, sorcerers, and idolaters we find the words "all liars." The text says that they "shall have their part in the lake which burns with fire and brimstone, which is the second death" (Revelation 21:8).

As we think about God and lying, of course, just the opposite of God is Satan, of whom the Bible says is "the father of lies." John 8:44 says that Satan "...was a murderer from the beginning, and does not stand in the truth, because *there is no truth in him*. When he speaks a lie, he speaks from his own resources, for he is a liar and the father of it."

MAN AND LYING

Let's change gears and think about man and lying. Proverbs 13:5 says, "A righteous man hates lying." As already mentioned, John 8:44 states that Satan is the father of lies. Someone has suggested, "A man is never more like the Devil than when he's telling a lie." Ponder that a moment. Do you think that's a true statement? In John 8, the Jews lied, and Jesus said, "You're just like your father. You are **of** the Devil."

Lying by the numbers

"The average person lies 25 times per day."

Lying is perhaps one of the most common of all sins. Recall that the average person lies twenty-five times a day. Can you think of another sin that is committed that often? Someone suggested that lusting might be more frequent. A person can do that from a distance and without even having another person present. Still, lying would have to be near the top of the list for its frequency because lying is a sin that plagues everyone from the very young to the very old. It is a sin that nearly every human who has ever lived any length of time on this earth has committed. But lying seems to be a bigger problem for some than for others. Some have reached the point where lying is *not* a trap that they fall into sometimes, but rather it is a way of life. At times the habitual liar will tell a lie when telling the truth would have been easier. It has been said about some people that you know they are lying "when their lips are moving."

What are some reasons why people lie? Sometimes people lie to get gain. A person might lie on his taxes in order to keep more of his money. A salesman might lie to a customer about a product to make a sale. Some might argue, "Oh, that's just business. You can't make a living in the car business if you don't fudge the truth a little bit!" If that is true, then that person better get out of the car business, because he can't go to Heaven if he continues to lie.

A man looking for a job might lie to the potential employer about his credentials in order to be hired. Another might lie to his employer by calling in and claiming to be sick when he actually just wants to take a day off. Worse yet, people will brag about this sort of thing!

There was a country music song several years ago called "I Don't Have to Be Me ('til Monday)," in which the artist sings, "So I called in to where I work, told a little white lie. No my back don't really hurt, but that's my alibi." And then he plans to go party. Though it's a song, it represents a common reality and a very accepted sin in our society. Proverbs 21:6, however, says, "Getting treasures by a lying tongue is the fleeting fantasy of those who seek death." In other words, those who get gain by lying are seeking eternal death. They will spend eternity in Hell because they lied in order to obtain temporary treasure now.

Another reason why people might lie is to keep themselves out of trouble. We see this in children caught with their hand in  the cookie jar. We see this with adults who might lie to the police. They are stopped for some traffic violation, and they may deny it altogether, or concoct some fabrication like, "I'm late picking up my child from school," or "I'm on my way to the hospital." There are a million "reasons" that people can come up with to keep themselves out of trouble. And again, all the way up to the highest government officials, we see them lying before Congress to avoid punishment for their actions. They play word games (semantics) to try to turn a lie into something other than a lie. It's repulsive to God, and *should* be repulsive to man, too.

Sometimes people lie to avoid hurting others' feelings. Do you suppose that Jesus engaged in that practice? We know that he did not, or else he would have ceased to be God, because God cannot lie.

To many people, this type of lying just wouldn't be that big of a deal. It is one of those sins we accept. We have even come up with a term for it, "little white lie." It's small. It is white (pure, innocent) and it doesn't hurt anybody and may actually spare some pain.

The Andy Griffith show is favorite show of this author, but frequently the blundering deputy, Barney Fife, botches up a situation, and Andy lies to spare his friend's feelings. Our society has reached the point where we think this is admirable. It is honorable because, after all, it was done because you care about people. We need, however, to realize that *lying is wrong*. It is a transgression of the law of God. We must not allow ourselves to measure sin by how much damage it does or does not do on this earth.

> ## Measuring Sin
> We must not allow ourselves to measure sin by how much damage it does or does not do on this earth.

Any sin can cause a man or woman to be lost and, in light of that, none of them are little. And too, the nature of a lie is that it grows. When one tells one lie, another must be told to cover it up. Someone once said, "If you never tell a lie, you never have to remember what you said."

As we think about man and lying, it is imperative that we realize lying is very costly. Lying hurts people. There is an old story about a little boy who had a problem with telling lies, so his father wanted to teach him a lesson. The father got a brand-new piece of wood and he drove ten nails into the wood. He then called his son and said to him, "Son, you have recently told ten lies. I want you to go back and fix them. For each one you correct, we will remove a nail from the wood." So the little boy set about to "fix" his lies. When he had finished and the tenth nail was pulled from the wood, the boy's father said, "Well, how does it look?" The boy responded, "The nails are gone, but the scars are still in the wood." His father said, "Now you have learned the lesson."

Lying does damage that is sometimes impossible to correct. It hurts feelings and scars reputations. A young girl in a small town high school once made accusations of a sexual nature against one of the male teachers. His reputation was destroyed, and it caused tremendous damage to his family. Finally the man was forced to move away to find another job. After some time had passed, the girl came forward and said, "I lied. It never really happened." Did her confession fix the problem? Did it undo the damage done? It did not.

Not only can lying hurt other people, it can ruin the liar's own reputation. Proverbs 22:1 says, "A good name is rather to be chosen than great riches..." The loss of one's good name is a tremendous loss indeed, and a surefire way to lose one's good name is to become a liar. Few people have respect for a liar, but a man who always tells the truth is esteemed almost everywhere.

A man is only as good as his word.

The old expression says, "A man is only as good as his word." Can you think of someone who you know that when he makes a promise, you are absolutely certain it will happen? His word is as good as gold. When a person achieves this kind of reputation he has a great treasure indeed. "A good name is rather to be chosen than great riches..."

As Christians, our personal reputations and commitment to the Lord should mean more to us than a brief gain we may get by lying. When you as a child of God reach the point where people can come to you as a Christian and know that you will always tell them the truth, whether it is pleasant or not, you have an invaluable treasure.

Lying can hurt other people. It can destroy your reputation, and it can hurt the church. If a man lives a doctrinally correct life, but not a morally correct one, he is living an inconsistent life. If a man will fight for the truth on baptism and the one church of the New Testament, but in his day-to-day life, he tells lies, what does that do to the church? Few things harm the Lord's church more than a man who claims to be a Christian and then doesn't live like one.

There have even been times in history when lying has cost a man his very life. In 1 Kings 13 we read the account of the young and old prophets. God sent the young prophet to speak against King Jeroboam and his idolatry. When he completed his task, God instructed the young man to not eat bread or drink water and to return home a different way. The old prophet, however, came to the young prophet inviting him come to his house for food. The young prophet knew better, but the old prophet argued that an angel said that it was okay. But then 1 Kings 13:18 adds these words, "But he lied unto him." The young prophet believed the lie, went home with the older prophet and was later killed by a lion as punishment for his disobedience to God. Believing a lie cost him his life.

In Acts 5 the Lord showed His disdain for lying when a man named Ananias and his wife Sapphira lied about a piece of property they had sold. They claimed they were giving all of the profit to the church, but in reality they kept back part of the money for themselves. They may have thought, "It's no big deal. We gave money to help the work of the Lord; we only lied about the percentage. It didn't hurt anybody, right?" Is this not the way we think sometimes today? But God made a powerful statement about how He regards lying, and struck both of them dead.

And the most important point of them all - *Lying can cost a man his soul*. Proverbs 21:6 says that a lying tongue is a characteristic of them that seek death. Revelation 21:8 says that all liars shall have their part in the second death (in the lake that burns with fire and brimstone). Second Thessalonians 2:12 teaches that *believing* a lie can cost men their souls. Many think of lying as insignificant and call it

Chapter 5 53

"little" and "white," but the reality is it can cause them to lose their most valuable possession, eternity with God.

CONCLUSION

Concerning God and lying, God cannot lie. He hates lying, and He forbids His children to lie. Lying is contrary to God's nature, but the Devil is the father of the lie. Like one man said, "Perhaps a man is never more like the Devil than when he is telling a lie."

Concerning man and lying, lying can hurt other people. It destroys reputations, and does untold damage to the church. Lying has cost men their lives and more importantly, their souls. Proverbs 12:22 says, "Lying lips are an abomination to the Lord, but they that deal truly are His delight."

Video Resources

THE TRUTH ABOUT... LYING (PART 1)

This video covers the controversial topic of lying. Should we lie to try and benefit ourselves or others?

TheTruthAbout.net/video/Lying-Part1

Lying

Part 2

Lying is always wrong. Colossians 3:9 says, "Lie not to one another." Proverbs 12:22 says, "Lying lips are an abomination to the Lord, but they that deal truly are His delight."

These verses and many others teach us that God hates lying. The Bible is very plain about this, so it is surprising when Christians try to defend lying. Unfortunately, it happens quite often. Their argument usually consists of some difficult situation with very serious consequences, and the person will suggest that in light of these very undesirable circumstances, lying is the better choice, and that God would even approve. Sometimes they will make appeals to events in the Bible that they believe imply that lying is permissible.

This study will cover three points. First, we will consider some of the scenarios (dilemmas) that people bring up to try to defend lying. Second, we will examine some of the Bible passages that people believe justify lying, and finally, we will list proof-positive Bible arguments that show that it is never right to lie.

SCENARIOS IN DEFENSE OF LYING

In an effort to defend lying, one individual brought up a situation in the area where he lives. Someone had been breaking into houses and committing rape. A grandfather was home alone with his two granddaughters. He heard something downstairs and, knowing about the crimes that had been taking place, told his granddaughters to hide while he went downstairs to investigate.

When the grandfather got downstairs, a man knocked him to the ground and put a gun to his head, asking, "Is there anyone else in the house?" The individual telling the story wanted to know, "What would *you* say? If you tell the truth, it is going to be tragedy for your granddaughters."

This individual then went on to suggest than under these extreme circumstances, it would be acceptable to lie. What answer would you give to the man's scenario? Admittedly, this is a terrible situation, one we hope never to encounter, but a wrong action does not turn into a right one just because the consequences are severe. Sin does not change to righteousness just because of an undesirable outcome. To reason otherwise is known as situational ethics. Situational ethics is when right or wrong is determined by the difficulty of the circumstance rather than objective truth.

Let's reconsider the story of the grandfather and the man with the gun, and let's alter the situation to suppose that the man who broke into the house is a psychopath who hates Christians. He pulls a gun on the old man and says, "I despise Christians with every bone in my body. Nothing pleases me more than to make them suffer. If you are a Christian, I'm going to make you suffer, and your granddaughters too. Do you believe Jesus Christ is the Son of God?"

We would ask, "What should a Christian to do in such a situation?" A defender of situational lying said, "Well, I would never lie about my Lord." We ask, why not? If it is true, as some argue, that God approves of lying to avoid suffering or to protect life, then why not lie? Though his conclusion was right, the way he arrived at that conclusion was wrong. When we practice situational ethics, we become our own god. Based upon our own judgment we determine what is worthy of a lie and what is not. The fact is, lying is never right in the sight of God, whether to protect life or not.

Abraham once lied to protect his own life. In Genesis 20, Abraham lied to Abimelech about his wife Sarah being his sister. The excuse he used was, "Because I thought, surely the fear of God is not in this place; and they will kill me on account of my wife." But despite the fact that he lied to protect his life, it is clear that God was not pleased with his actions.

Another argument someone has posed to justify lying is "If lying is always wrong, then the government could not lie, and if the government cannot lie, then that puts our spies and intelligence programs in serious jeopardy."

It is true that many governments lie (shocking as that may seem) and sometimes convince themselves that it is necessary to do so. But the Bible still says, "Let your 'Yes' be 'Yes,' and your 'No,' 'No.' For whatever is more than these is from the evil one" (Matthew 5:37). Proverbs 14:34 says, "Righteousness exalts a nation, but sin is a reproach to any people." If a government lies, it is not right just because it's the government. Again, the consequences of a sin do not somehow transform it into a "non-sin."

In the same context, someone even suggested that "the truth is so precious that sometimes it has to be protected by a bodyguard of lies." This is absolute nonsense! That is the Devil's handiwork. The Bible says, "Buy the truth and sell it not..." (Proverbs 23:23). Don't ever be the one who gives up holding onto truth. There is nothing so precious upon this earth that one should cease to walk in the pathway of truth, and instead walk down the pathway of the Devil.

Someone said, "Always tell the truth. If you can't always tell the truth, don't lie." Sometimes in difficult situations, the best thing to do is say nothing.

Sometimes men will even argue that mercy overrides truth, that mercy is greater than truth, and that being the case, there are times when we must lie in order to uphold mercy. But that begs the question: if lying is justified by mercy, does mercy also justify other sins? Could adultery be justified by mercy? Could homosexuality? Could abortion? Could we indeed have such a thing as "mercy killings?"

> ## Tell the Truth
> *Always tell the truth. If you can't always tell the truth, don't lie.*

God is a God known for His mercy. Ephesians 2:4 says He is "rich in mercy" and yet Titus 1:2 says He "cannot lie." The two are not mutually exclusive; they do not contradict each other. Certainly, no one would ever question the wonderful mercy of Christ (Titus 1:4, Jude 21), and yet we never read about Jesus lying. Is it the case that we are faced with moral dilemmas which would demand that we choose the lesser of two evils, and yet the Lord never was? If He never was, what about Hebrews 4:15 which says, "He was tempted in all points like as we are..."

When the Lord walked on this earth, He set the perfect example for us to emulate. We can fabricate all of the scenarios we want, but let's ask, "What would the Lord do if He were in these dilemmas?" Certainly He would not lie because if He did, at that moment, He would cease to be God. Titus 1:2 says God cannot lie. Jesus said, "I am the way, the truth, and the life" (John 14:6).

SUPPOSED "BIBLICAL" JUSTIFICATION FOR LYING

Perhaps one of the most common arguments brought up to justify lying for a good cause is an appeal to the story of Rahab. One person posed it this way, "When the spies entered the Promised Land to spy out the land, what would have happened if Rahab had not lied and protected them? How would the children of Israel have received the Promised Land?" The answer is easy: "God would have done it some other way." Romans 8:28 says, "All things work together for good to them that love God." This passage is teaching us that, regardless of

what men may do to us, or what may happen to us, God can use it to accomplish His will. God's plan was not dependent upon Rahab. He would have accomplished what He wanted done whether or not she lied.

Sometimes it is arugued, "When the spies came to Rahab, she lied to protect them. Later she was blessed for her actions; therefore we have a situation where a lie met with God's approval. Thus, it was a justified lie." Let's read the passage and see. The story is in Joshua 2:1-7: "Now Joshua the son of Nun sent out two men from Acacia Grove to spy secretly, saying, 'Go, view the land, especially Jericho.' So they went, and came to the house of a harlot named Rahab, and lodged there. And it was told the king of Jericho, saying, 'Behold, men have come here tonight from the children of Israel to search out the country.' So the king of Jericho sent to Rahab, saying, 'Bring out the men who have come to you, who have entered your

Lying Part 2

house, for they have come to search out all the country.' Then the woman took the two men and hid them. So she said, 'Yes, the men came to me, but I did not know where they were from. And it happened as the gate was being shut, when it was dark, that the men went out. Where the men went I do not know; pursue them quickly, for you may over take them.' (But she had brought them up to the roof and hidden them with the stalks of flax, which she had laid in order on the roof). Then the men pursued them by the road to the Jordan, to the fords. And as soon as those who pursued them had gone out, they shut the gate."

When reading this account, it is clear that Rahab did lie. She actually lied several times. In verse 4 she says, "I did not know where they were from." She says in verse 5, "When it was dark, the men went out," and also, "Where the men went, I do not know." The problem seems to arise when we get to the New Testament and see that Rahab is actually complimented by God for her behavior. Some think this is sanction for lying.

Let's consider the two passages in the New Testament that mention Rahab. Hebrews 11:31 says, "By faith the harlot Rahab did not perish with those who did not believe, when she received the spies with peace." Where does this passage condone lying? It doesn't. Rahab is simply complimented for receiving the spies peacefully.

The second passage is James 2:25, which says, "Likewise, was not Rahab the harlot also justified by works when she received the messengers and sent them out another way?" Again, this Scripture does not applaud her lying. One person tried to argue from this passage that lying was an inherent part of "sending them out another way." But please appreciate that this passage can stand wholly and separately apart from the lie. Let's assume that it took place this way: the king's men came to the house, knocked on the door and said, "Can we come in and look around?"

What About Rahab?
Rahab's lies are never condoned in the Scriptures.

And Rahab said, "Sure," so they came in, walked around, found nothing and left. Under these circumstances, could the Scriptures have complimented her for receiving them and sending them out

Chapter 6   **59**

another way? Yes! The statement is not then dependent upon the lie. Rahab's lies are never condoned in the Scriptures. The story about Rahab merely provides an example of where God honored a woman because of her obedient faith, in spite of many character flaws. At the time, she was a heathen, a harlot, and a liar, but she tried to help God's people. God thus blesses her, in spite of character flaws, not because of them.

Another passage people sometimes appeal to in order to justify lying is Exodus 1:15-22. This is an account of the Hebrew midwives. It says, "Then the king of Egypt spoke to the Hebrew midwives, of whom the name of one was Shiphrah and the name of the other Puah; and he said, 'When you do the duties of a midwife for the Hebrew women, and see them on the birthstools, if it is a son, then you shall kill him; but if it is a daughter, then she shall live.' But the midwives feared God, and did not do as the king of Egypt commanded them, but saved the male children alive. So the king of Egypt called for the midwives and said to them, 'Why have you done this thing, and saved the male children alive?' And the midwives said to Pharaoh, 'Because the Hebrew women are not like the Egyptian women; for they are lively and give birth before the midwives come to them.' Therefore God dealt well with the midwives, and the people multiplied and grew very mighty. And so it was, because the midwives feared God, that He provided households for them. So Pharaoh commanded all his people, saying, 'Every son who is born you shall cast into the river, and every daughter you shall save alive.' "

The argument goes like this: Pharaoh commanded the midwives to kill the newborn male Hebrews. The midwives disobeyed the decree. The midwives lied when questioned concerning their actions. God blessed the midwives. Since God blessed the action of which a lie was a part, He must have sanctioned a lie.

This is false, and not what the Bible says. The text tells us that God blessed the midwives *because they feared Him*, not because they lied. Verse 17 indicates that the way they exhibited their fear of God was by sparing the babies, and that was prior to the lie even taking place. The midwives spared the babies because they feared God. They lied because they feared Pharaoh. There is no justification for lying in this passage.

Another Bible passage where people will sometimes seek justification for lying is 1 Samuel 16:1-2. In this chapter God has rejected Saul from being the king and has instructed the prophet Samuel to anoint a new king from among the sons of Jesse the Bethlehemite. Samuel is concerned about this, because he asks, "What if King Saul hears about this? He'll kill me." So in verse 2, the Bible says, "And the Lord said, 'Take a heifer with you, and say, 'I have come to sacrifice to the Lord.'" And so the argument suggests that God actually told Samuel to lie in order to protect himself from Saul. In reality it wasn't a lie at all. As we continue on in the chapter, we see that God instructed Samuel to arrange a sacrifice in Bethlehem and to invite the family of Jesse to the sacrifice. At the occasion of that sacrifice, God would reveal to Samuel which one of the sons was to be the next king, and he would anoint him there. It was not a lie at all.

A very desperate argument has even been made concerning the wise men in Matthew 2. It has been suggested that they lied by not returning to Herod after they saw the baby Jesus. Listen to what Matthew 2:7-8 says, "Then Herod, when he had privily called the wise men, inquired of them diligently what time the star appeared. And he sent them to Bethlehem, and said, 'Go and search diligently for the young child; and when ye have found him, bring me word again, that I may come and worship him also.' When they had heard the king, they departed." The Scriptures say nothing about the wise men's promising to return. Besides that, in verse 12 God told them to go a different way. There is certainly no justification for lying in these verses.

LYING IS ALWAYS WRONG

Proof #1: Right and Wrong are not determined by earthly consequences.

Some of these proofs have already been alluded to, but now we want to put them together here in a neat package. The first proof that shows that lying is always wrong is that right and wrong are not determined by earthly consequences. Sometimes doing right is very costly. Jesus told the rich young ruler that doing right would cost him all he had. Doing right cost the apostle Paul beatings and abuse. When we begin to determine right and wrong based on the earthly consequences, we are going to get really out of whack. First John 3:4 says, "Whosoever commits sin transgresses also the law: for sin is the transgression of the law." This is how we determine right and wrong, not by the severity of consequences.

Proof #2: Revelation 2:10

Revelation 2:10 says, "Be faithful unto death and I will give you a crown of life." This passage was written to Christians who were suffering persecution. The beginning of verse 10 discusses the fact that they were going to suffer. Some of them would be thrown into prison and undergo tribulation. It is in this context that the Lord says, "Be faithful unto death." Homer Hailey, in his commentary on Revelation, phrased it this way, "even to the point of dying."

What is the Lord saying? "Be faithful and do right, even if it costs you your life." This destroys the scenarios that suggest that lying is justified to protect life. The truth is more precious than life itself. God is the God of truth (Psalm 31:5), and we as Christians want to be like Him. Remember that Jesus said in Matthew 10:28, "Fear not him who can destroy the body and not the soul, but rather fear Him Who is able to destroy both the body and soul in hell." Jesus is saying, "Don't be afraid of physical death; be afraid of sinning and losing your soul."

Proof #3: Revelation 21:8

Revelation 21:8 says, "All liars shall have their part in the lake that burns with fire and brimstone, which is the second death." It does not say "some liars." It does not say "All, except those who were put in really tough situations." It does not say, "All, except those who lied to protect human life." It simply says, "All." People can come up with all the hypothetical, extreme situations they want, but what they really need, if they want to win the argument that says lying is acceptable, is a passage of Scripture where God says it is all right to lie. There isn't one.

Proof #4: Titus 1:2

Titus 1:2 clearly states God cannot lie. If lying were really acceptable sometimes, why can't God do it? Why did Jesus Christ never do it? If mercy justifies lying, why can't the God of mercy lie? The answer is that lying is inherently evil. It is *always wrong*. That is why God cannot it.

Proof #5: Satan is the source of lying

Satan is the originator of lying. John 8:44 says, "You are of your father the devil, and the desires of your father you want to do. He was a murderer from the beginning, and does not stand in the truth, because there is not truth in him. When he speaks a lie, he speaks from his own resources, for he is a liar, and the father of it."

When the devil tells a lie, he speaks from his own resources. Again, Matthew 5:37 says, "Let your 'Yes' be 'Yes,' and your 'No,' 'No.' For whatever is more than these is from the evil one."

When people lie, their father is the devil. He is the source of lies. To suggest that it is sometimes acceptable to lie is equivalent to saying that it is sometimes acceptable to stop following God and to follow Satan instead. We reject this conclusion with every fiber of our being.

Matthew 5:37
But let your 'Yes' be 'Yes' and your 'No,' 'No'. For whatever is more than these is from the evil one.

Proof #6: God will provide a way of escape.

It has been offered by someone seeking to defend lying that sometimes one must choose the lesser of two evils. When faced with statements such as this, we need to remember 1 Corinthians 10:13, "God is faithful, Who will not allow you to be tempted beyond what you are able, but with the temptation will also make the way of escape, that you may be able to bear it."

We can trust that God's way of escape from sin is not going to be another sin! There will always be a path we can choose which does not involve violating God's will. A person may not always choose God's way, but it is there nonetheless.

CONCLUSION

Thinking that it is all right to lie is a very serious error for a Christian to hold. It shows a misunderstanding of God Himself. Proverbs 6:17 says, "God hates the lying tongue." Proverbs 12:22 says, "Lying lips are an abomination to the Lord, but they that deal truly are His delight." Psalm 31:5 calls God, the God of truth. The psalmist wrote, "For the word of the Lord is right; and all His words are done in truth" (Psalm 33:4). We also read in Leviticus 19:11, "You shall not steal, neither deal falsely, neither lie to one another." Proverbs 13:5 says, "A righteous man hates lying." Lying is **always** wrong.

Video Resources

THE TRUTH ABOUT... LYING (PART 2)

 This video covers the controversial topic of lying. Should we lie to stay out of trouble or to gain an advantage?

<u>TheTruthAbout.net/video/Lying-Part2</u>

MODESTY

If you've been to the mall recently, turned on the television, or even looked at a billboard while riding down the road, then you know that our country has a problem with the way we clothe ourselves. Sexually provocative is the way of the day. Less is considered better. It would be an understatement to say that the world is confused about how we should dress. The cartoon on the next page illustrates the point. The doorbell rings. One girl says, "Oh dear, that's the doorbell, and here I am in my underclothes." The other girl (who is wearing far less) says, "I'm dressed. I'll get it." Our society doesn't understand modesty.

People are no longer embarrassed about the exposure of their bodies. We are bombarded these days with commercials about dieting, the theme of which is being able to display our bodies. One commerical depicts the tiny bikini hanging in the wall. It's the woman's motivation to lose weight. She's not embarrassed to display a nearly nude body: it's her goal! The prophet Jeremiah said the people of his day had lost the ability to blush: "Were they ashamed when they had committed abomination? No! They were not at all ashamed; nor did they know how to blush" (Jeremiah 6:15). We live in a world just like that. Many people have lost the ability to blush over the exposure of their bodies. One preacher said, "I would like to find out what kind of fruit Adam and Eve ate that made them realize they were naked, because I'd like to pass it around again." The statement is tongue-in-cheek, but the preacher was right, because many people need to have their eyes opened to what is appropriate and what is inappropriate.

The world has it wrong with regard to how we should clothe ourselves, but a Christian is not like the world. A Christian cannot be like the world. We are different! We have been called out of the world. First John 2:15 says, "Do not love the world or the things in the world. If anyone loves the world, the love of the Father is not in him." Romans 12:2 says, "And do not be conformed to this world, but be transformed by the renewing of your mind, that you may prove what is that good and acceptable and perfect will of God."

Sadly, the problem of immodesty (lack of clothing) has affected many Christians and has crept into the church. In some congregations men do not want to serve at the Lord's table because of young ladies who are immodestly dressed in worship. Some wives do not want their husbands to teach teenagers because of the way some of the girls are dressed—or maybe not dressed.

Modesty is an unpleasant subject to discuss and sometimes

embarrassing both to the teacher and to the audience. Sometimes those who like to dress immodestly get angry because they feel as if they are being insulted. Sometimes when people teach on this subject, others will accuse them of having dirty minds. Because of the anger it provokes, some would rather just avoid the issue altogether. They feel it is just not worth the grief. But if we are going to be pleasing to God, the matter must be discussed. We have to get this right!

Whether or not we want to admit it, when a woman goes into public in a modern swimming suit, mini-skirt, or shorts; with her midriff showing; or wearing clothing that is too tight, she is doing something sinful. She is corrupting (cheapening) the sexual impulses that God instilled in men to draw husbands and wives together. She may not even know she is doing it, but she is distorting sex as God designed it.

Why is it the case that the man is sexually impressed by the woman? It is not an accident. God made him that way. Why? Genesis 2:24 says, "Therefore shall a man leave his father and his mother, and shall cleave unto his wife: and they shall be one flesh." The reason man is sexually impressed by and attracted to woman is because of God's design. However, there is a big difference in the physical attraction of a husband and wife, and that of a man who is physically attracted to a stranger at the beach, at the pool, or at the mall.

First, consider at the husband/wife relationship.

Let your fountain be blessed, And rejoice with the wife of your youth. As a loving deer and a graceful doe, Let her breasts satisfy you at all times; And always be enraptured with her love (Proverbs 5:18-19).

Contrast this to the unmarried man/woman.

But I say to you that whoever looks at a woman to lust for her has already committed adultery with her in his heart (Matthew 5:28).

Someone may try to rationalize and say, "Well, so long as nothing physical happens, there's nothing wrong with it." Another commonly stated expression is, "It's all right to look so long as you don't touch." But that is not right! The Bible teaches that God is concerned not only about our actions, but also with our hearts (Matthew 5:28). Job said, "I have made a covenant with my eyes; why then should I look upon a young woman?" (Job 31:1). Job

Job 31:1
I have made a covenant with my eyes; why then should I look upon a young woman?

understood it would be wrong to even look at a woman in a lustful manner. This matter of properly clothing ourselves is certainly important, and the world is quite confused about it, so here are some considerations to help guide us in knowing how we should dress.

MODESTY

GOD'S LAW

Sometimes people will say, "The Bible doesn't really tell us how to dress ourselves." That is not true; the Bible does tell us. Let's begin in Genesis 2:25 where the Bible says about Adam and Eve, "They were both naked, the man and his wife, and were not ashamed." Why were they not ashamed? Because they were not aware of the fact they were naked (3:7). After they ate of the forbidden fruit, Adam's and Eve's eyes were opened, and they were made aware of their condition. Then they sewed fig leaves together and made themselves aprons or, as the New King James Version says, "coverings." This word means "a girdle or a loin cloth." One version states they covered "themselves around the hips." What is very interesting is that the clothing they made was apparently not adequate according to God's standards, for the Bible says "Also for Adam and his wife the Lord God made tunics of skin, and clothed them" (3:21). The Hebrew word for tunic means "a long shirt-like garment." Strong's Concordance even gives the definition "a robe." It was a garment that began at the shoulders and flowed down like a long shirt. Adam and Eve had made themselves

The First Clothes
Adam and Eve made "loin coverings" of leaves; God made them "robes of skin."

"loin coverings", but the Lord made them "robes" and "clothed them." The implication seems to be that they were not sufficiently covered by the fig leaves alone. Notice also when God came into the garden, Adam said, "I was naked and hid myself." He had on fig leaves, but he still refers to himself as being naked, and God did not argue with him! God simply replied with, "Who told you that you were naked?" God affirms that Adam was naked while wearing the loin covering.

Secondly, consider Exodus 28. This chapter tells about the making of the priests' garments under the Mosaic system. Exodus 28:40-42 says:

For Aaron's sons you shall make tunics, and you shall make sashes for them. And you shall make hats for them, for glory and beauty. So shall you put them on Aaron your brother and on his sons with him. You shall anoint them, consecrate them, and sanctify them, that they may minister to Me as priests. And you shall make for them linen trousers to cover their nakedness; they shall reach from the waist to the thighs.

Notice especially the phrase, "they shall reach from the waist to the thighs." One version phrases it, "reaching from hips to knees." What was the purpose of this garment? The text says, "to cover their nakedness." Thomas Eaves, in his tract on modesty, wrote, "In the Old Testament it was considered nakedness when one uncovered the thighs." Mr. Eaves cites Exodus 28:42 as proof for his statement. To summarize: *In order to be adequately covered, clothing started at the shoulders and went down to the knees.*

A third passage relating to how we should clothe ourselves is 1 Timothy 2:9-10: "In like manner also, that the women adorn themselves in modest apparel, with propriety and moderation, not with braided hair or gold or pearls or costly clothing, but, which is proper for women professing godliness, with good works."

We need to notice three things in these verses. First, the word *modest*. This word means "orderly, well-arranged, or decent." The idea is that the woman is to adorn or beautify herself in a way that avoids drawing undue attention to herself. In the immediate context, the writer is discussing is a woman who is overdoing it; someone who is wearing flashy clothes, too much makeup, and an excessive amount of jewelry.

But there is another way in which a woman could draw undue attention to herself: by underdoing it, by wearing too little. When she wears clothes that are too tight, too short, too thin, too little, or too revealing, a woman is violating this Christian principle.

The second word to consider is *propriety* (The King James Version uses *shamefacedness*). The word *propriety* is actually closer to our modern word *modest*. The Greek word for shamefacedness means, "a sense of shame, modesty used regarding the demeanor of women in the church."

The third phrase is in verse 10: "but, which is proper for women professing godliness." Additionally, notice that Titus 2 states that older women are to teach the younger women to be *chaste*. This word means "pure from carnality, modest, perfect, innocent" (Strong's and Vine's definitions combined). Now let's pull it all together. A godly woman is to dress in such a way as to avoid drawing undue attention to herself. She should have a sense of shame or modesty about her. She should be innocent and pure from carnality, and she should dress as a woman whose most important object in life is to please God.

Sadly, modern-day swimwear does not fit this description. A person who wants to please the Lord has no business being out in public in swimwear. (That would include both bikinis and one-piece bathing suits.) Cut-off shirts that expose the midriff do not mesh with God's standards. Most modern-day cheer leading uniforms don't even come remotely close to fitting the description

of a woman professing godliness. And modesty is not determined by the environment. Participating in a sporting event, attending a wedding, or being near water does not change immodest into modest. Even hot weather does not transform immodest into modest. On one occasion, a woman came to speak to President Woodrow Wilson about some matter. When the woman had left, another man in the office mentioned something to the President about her being an attractive and intelligent woman. President Wilson replied, "She was a well-dressed woman." The other man said, "I didn't notice what she was wearing." President Wilson answered, "That's how I know she was well dressed."

Some people may say, "You're talking a lot about the woman, but isn't modesty applicable to the man as well?" Indeed, it is. When you read the Bible, it's interesting though that principles of modesty are applied to women, and passages prohibiting lust are applied to men. Is that because women never lust, or because modesty doesn't apply to men? No. It's because of the way human beings are designed. Lust is generally a bigger

MODESTY

problem for the man than for the woman, but the principles of modesty also apply to men. If a man goes into public with his shirt unbuttoned halfway down his chest, or wearing no shirt at all, or in skin-tight jeans, he is doing something sinful and can, no doubt, be a stumbling block for women.

This leads us to our next point. Our first consideration with regard to our clothing must be God. Our second consideration should be other people.

OTHER PEOPLE

A second principle to guide us in determining how we should dress is what effect our clothing (or lack thereof) has on other people. If a Christian is living so as to please the Lord, he or she doesn't want to do anything that would cause someone else to sin. He or she doesn't want to be a stumbling block in other people's paths. As it is, the way one clothes oneself or does not clothe oneself can be a stumbling block for others which may lead them into sin. Jesus said in Matthew 5:28, "Whoever looks at a woman to lust for her has already committed adultery with her in his heart." Did you know that you can commit a sin in your mind that can cause you to lose your soul? That is exactly what the Lord teaches us in this verse.

With this in mind, when a person is purchasing clothing, he or she needs to think about other people and what effect it may have on them. One author wrote, "The leading fashion designers admit that the reason behind the short skirts and bare skin is to seduce the men." But a faithful Christian would not and should not want to do that. Consider Jesus' words in Luke 17:1, "It is impossible that no offense should come, but woe to him through whom they do come!" One translation says, "How terrible to him for whom they come." We do not want to be the cause of other people's stumbling.

Fashion Motives
The leading fashion designers admit that the reason behind the short skirts and bare skin is to seduce the men.

MODESTY

A survey was done among high school boys in which they were asked the following questions:

- Can a girl tempt a boy by the way she dresses?
  98% of the boys answered "Yes."
- Does fashion use sex appeal?
  96% percent said "Yes."
- Do you believe that boys are stimulated by sight more than girls?
  92% percent said "Yes."
- Do you believe the passions of boys are: (A) More easily aroused than girls? (B) Less easily aroused? (C) Same?
  87% answered "(A) – More easily aroused."
- Do you feel that girls really understand the problem of immodest apparel?
  50% said "No."
- Which part of the female body as seen in public most quickly arouses your emotions?
  60% said "Legs."
- If you were married, would you want other men and boys to lust after your wife?
  96% percent said "No."
- If she dressed like most girls do today, would most boys be tempted to lust after her?
  77% said "Yes."

What does this survey tell us? The way we dress can and does affect those around us!

Sometimes people say, "Well, it doesn't matter how I dress or don't dress, people are going to sin or they're not going to sin." Consider for a moment 2 Samuel 11. King David is walking on the roof of the king's house, and he sees Bathsheba washing herself, evidently unclothed to some degree. The Bible says, "She was very beautiful to look upon." David sent for her and committed adultery with her. If Bathsheba had been completely covered in a godly manner, would she have had the same effect on David? The answer is obviously no. It is a fact that the way we dress can tempt individuals in ways they would not otherwise be tempted.

Some people will argue, "It's the person lusting who is sinning, not me," or "Evil is in the eye of the beholder." First,

MODESTY

this is not true, and secondly, if it were true, it shows a very low regard for the souls of others. Thirdly, it is not even a logical argument. If "evil is in the eye of the beholder" as people say, then it would be fine for a person to go out in public completely nude, and the only ones doing wrong would be those looking.

If a female (or male) has concern for the spiritual well-being of others, she should be careful how she dresses. The following is an excerpt from a church bulletin:

Dear sisters, on behalf of and for the benefit of men who are seeking to live in accordance with the will of God and to keep themselves pure and holy, to the end that you not encourage them to lust, and for your own eternal welfare, please do not call undue attention to yourself or expose yourself by wearing immodest apparel. Godly men do not want to see your thighs (or more) in clothing that is too short, your cleavage in tops that are too low, your navels in tops that are too short, your undergarments in clothing that is too thin, nor the curves and characteristics of your bodies in clothing that is too tight. Please look in the mirror at yourself (front and back) and ask yourself if your attire is becoming one professing godliness. You may need to make some changes.

Remember the Lord said, "Whoever looks at a woman to lust for her has already committed adultery with her in his heart." In light of this, we need to consider other people when we are choosing our clothing.

THE CHURCH

For people who are members of the church, this is especially important, because people who wear the name Christian are representatives of the Lord's body. The way a Christian conducts himself reflects on the precious church of the Lord. There's a very interesting passage in 2 Corinthians 3:2 that says, "You are our epistle written in our hearts, known and read by all men." The apostle Paul is writing here that Christians are walking Bibles, living examples of Christ's teachings. When a Christian dresses immodestly he sends a corrupted message to the world.

Christians need to realize we are a holy people (1 Peter 1:15-16). As children of God we are to "set our mind on the things above, not on things on the earth." We must guard ourselves and not be "conformed to this world" (Romans 12:2).

When people know a member of the church of Christ, and they hear him stand for and defend the plan of salvation, what the Bible has to say about baptism, and the proper type of worship, but then see him in public dressed inappropriately, how will they view the church? When they hear him dogmatically defend doctrine, but then see him engage in practices that even much of the world views as sensual, how will they feel toward the body of Christ?

As we ponder how our clothing reflects on the church, consider the description of what Christ thinks about His church.

Husbands, love your wives, just as Christ also loved the church and gave Himself for her, that He might sanctify and cleanse her with the washing of water by the word, that He might present her to Himself a glorious church, not having spot or wrinkle or any such thing, but that she should be holy and without blemish (Ephesians 5:25-27).

FALSE IDEAS ABOUT IMMODEST CLOTHING

Some apparently hold to the idea that immodest clothing is acceptable if one is involved in a sporting event. The Bible does not, however, lay aside principles of modesty so that someone can win a swim meet, compete in gymnastics, or even be a cheerleader. If you have ever watched the Summer Olympics, you know that in some of the sports the clothing is nearly non-existent. For some strange reason, even people who would normally oppose 95 percent nudity don't have a problem with it at a sporting event! This is a false idea, and God does not make that exception. In the marriage relationship, it is appropriate to see each other so scantily clad. First Corinthians 7:4 says, "The wife does not have authority over her own body, but the husband does. And likewise the husband does not have authority over his own body, but the wife does." There is no verse that makes an exception for sporting events.

Sometimes it is argued that "people see so much nakedness these days that they just don't really pay any attention to it anymore." This argument is simply not true. A man might eat his favorite food until he becomes sick of it and loses his appetite for it, but God has not made us that way with reference to sexual desires. Besides, if that were the case, why do cheerleaders continue to wear skimpy uniforms in the dead of winter? It's not about team spirit!

False Arguments
1. "At sporting events it's OK."
2. "It doesn't bother me."
3. "They are just children."

Another false idea relates to our children. A parent might think, "But my daughter is just a child! Certainly she isn't the object of lust." Well, she may not be to the parent, but what about a boy her age? Parents, it happens very quickly that our little girls turn into little women, and that's when Daddy needs to step up to the spiritual headship that God gave him.

One preacher wrote, "There's not an ordinary man who can look at a woman clad in nothing but a bathing suit for a long time without entertaining evil thoughts." But some will say, 'It does not bother me.' One who says that may be so young that his passions have not arisen, or he may be so old that they have subsided, or he may be so ignorant that he doesn't know what is going on, or he may not he normal, or he may be lying. He fits into one of these five categories, or he is a spiritual giant; but spiritual giants don't spend their time at mixed swimming parties.

Some people have the idea that when a girl dresses immodestly, she is intentionally dressing to entice men. While that may be true of some women, it is not true for all of them. God has made us different. Men and women are wired differently with regard to sexual desires and many times, especially with young girls, they do not truly understand the effect their clothing has on those of the opposite sex. This is why a husband or father must take the spiritual lead with reference to what is worn by his wife and daughters.

CONCLUSION

How we clothe ourselves can have eternal implications both for us and for those around us. It can glorify God, or it can bring reproach on His church. The factors in choosing what to wear cannot hinge on, "Is this in style?" or "Is this comfortable?" or "Is this cool?" Our number one consideration must be, "Is this godly?" Eternally speaking, none of those other reasons are ever going to matter.

Video Resources

THE TRUTH ABOUT... MODESTY

This video covers the important topic of modesty. Can Christians wear anything a store sells? Do cultural norms change a Christian's perspective?

TheTruthAbout.net/video/Modesty

PORNOGRAPHY

Would you be surprised to learn that the majority of Internet pornography use occurs in the office place? Statistics indicate that 70 percent of all Internet pornography traffic occurs during the nine-to-five workday. According to IDC, a source of global marketing intelligence, 30 to 40 percent of Internet use in the workplace is unrelated to business. Nielsen/NetRating has determined that 21 percent of all adult sites are accessed from work. Meanwhile, 70 percent of employees surveyed by NFO Worldwide admit to viewing or sending adult-oriented emails at work.[1]

Pornography is one of those very uncomfortable subjects that people don't like to talk or preach about, but it is a very real issue that is destroying people's lives and marriages. Jesus addressed it in Matthew 5:28-29 when He said, "But I say to you that whoever looks at a woman to lust for her has already committed adultery with her in his heart. If your right eye causes you to sin, pluck it out and cast it from you; for it is more profitable for you that one of your members perish, than for your whole body to be cast into hell." The Lord warned us, but even still, pornography is a problem in the world and in the church.

Consider these statistics involing various religious groups. In December of 2000, the National Coalition to Protect Children and Families surveyed five Christian college campuses to see how the next generation of believers was doing with regard to sexual purity. Forty-eight percent of males admitted to current porn use and 68 percent of males said they had intentionally viewed a sexually explicit website at the school. A 1996 Promise Keepers survey conducted at one of their stadium events revealed that more than

> ## Sexual Purity
> 48% of males admitted to current porn use
>
> 68% said they viewed sexually explicit websites at school

PORNOGRAPHY

50 percent of the men in attendance had been involved with pornography within one week of attending the rally.[2] A CNN article by Jason Rovou dated April 6, 2007, stated that 70 percent of Christians admitted to struggling with pornography in their daily lives.[3]

Pornography is a real problem even for religious people. Someone might say, "It's different in the church of Christ," but sadly the problem exists even amongst members of the Lord's true church. There are Christians who attend worship on Sunday morning, then go home to their computers and engage in this secret sin.

In recent years, pornography has become even easier to access because of the Internet. There used to be a built-in deterrent, because one had to physically go somewhere to get it. And a trip to the store to buy a dirty magazine or video brought with the risk of being seen or

caught. The Internet has changed this, because now pornography is readily available in the privacy of one's home, and it can be accessed with total anonymity (or so it is thought). In fact, it has been said that the three "A's" of the Internet have caused the porn industry to explode with growth: Accessibility, Affordability, and Anonymity. We might add one more word – Addiction – and make it four "A's." These things have made the pornography industry reach record numbers worldwide.

Every second, 3,075.64 dollars are being spent on pornography. Every second, 28,258 Internet users are viewing pornography. Every second, 372 Internet users are typing adult search terms into search engines. Every 39 minutes, a new pornographic video is being created in the United States. The income from the pornography industry is larger than the revenues of the top technology companies combined: Microsoft, Google, Amazon, eBay, Yahoo!, Apple, Netflix, and EarthLink. According to a 2003 statistic on Internetfilterview.com, the sex industry brings in 57 billion dollars in revenue per year worldwide.[4] Of this amount, 12 billion is United States revenue, which is more than the combined revenues of professional football, baseball, and basketball franchises, or the combined revenues of ABC, CBS, and NBC (6.2 billion dollars). Roughly 2.5 of the 12 billion dollars are related to Internet porn.[5]

Where are we as a country? Barna Research Group did a survey in 2003 which indicated that 38 percent of adults believe it is morally acceptable to look at pictures of nudity or explicit sexual behavior. Fifty-nine percent of adults believe it is morally acceptable to have sexual thoughts or fantasies, and 38 percent of adults believe there is nothing wrong with pornography use.[6]

HOW DOES IT HAPPEN?

How do people first get exposed to and hooked on pornography? There's an element of this that is natural. Males are naturally stimulated by sight. This is the way God made them; however, that does not make pornography right. There is a proper outlet for this desire—the marriage relationship. But it is a fact that men are naturally stimulated by sight. Many times, women fail to understand and appreciate that fact.

In the book *Every Young Man's Battle*, the authors write, "Women seldom understand this because they aren't sexually stimulated in the same way. Their ignitions are tied to touch and relationship. They view this aspect of our sexuality as shallow." The wife of one of the authors even said, "When I first heard how men are, it seemed so wild and unlike anything I could imagine…I had a hard time believing it and occasionally even wondered if men were making it up." The writers continue, "Because women can't relate, they have little mercy on us and rarely choose to dress modestly."[7] Hopefully, that isn't true of Christian women!

Some have taken this built-in desire that God gave men and have perverted it. They have twisted it into something that God never intended. It's what we call pornography. *Pornography* comes from two Greek words: one is the word for "prostitute" and the other is the word for "I write" or "I record." Pornography refers to a written or illustrated depiction of prostitution.

When are people first exposed to pornography? Some people have said that they were first exposed to it in the form of magazines that they found under their dad's bed. In the book *Every Young Man's Battle*, one of the authors states that he first saw it in the form of posters of nude women in his grandfather's shop. These days, many are first exposed to it on the Internet.

In 2003, the average age at which children were first introduced to pornography by way of the Internet was 11 years old. Maybe now the age would be even younger. Also, the largest consumer of Internet pornography is the 12 to 17 age group.[5]

At first, it is shocking to them. On *Good Morning America* there was a segment about babies in the mother's womb, and their reaction when they were exposed to a loud noise. At first, the baby jumped because the noise startled him. But then as they continued to expose the child to the noise, the baby became used to it. The shock faded away. A similar thing happens with pornography. The more we view it, the more the shock diminishes. One porn

user stated, "Once you become addicted to it...you look for more potent, more explicit, more graphic kinds of material. Like an addiction, you keep craving something which is harder and gives you a greater sense of excitement, until you reach the point where the pornography only goes so far—that jumping off point where you begin to think maybe actually doing it will give you that which is just beyond reading about it and looking at it."[8]

Considering the sin involved in pornography, its addictive nature, and the fact that it is so easily accessible, concerned parents realize that precautions need to be taken with regard to their children. There are various pieces of software and programs available to help protect your family from pornography. One program, *Safe Eyes*, filters pornography and blocks inappropriate sites. It will even email the parents if their child tries to access a prohited site. Of course, we have to be careful of the TV as well. The average teenager spends three to four hours per day watching television, and 83 percent of the programming most frequently watched by adolescents contains sexual content. Thirty-nine million homes receive the adult channels in scrambled form, while the number of children with potential exposure to such images is about 29 million.[2]

Christian men, don't ever let it be said that your son was exposed to pornography because of you. It's a sin to subscribe to those adult channels anyway. It's a sin to own pornographic magazines. It's a sin to visit those websites. You can't go to heaven while indulging these sinful behaviors. Please don't risk the souls of your children! Beware of movie channels such as HBO and Showtime. Don't put those temptations before your children.

PORNOGRAPHY

THE EFFECTS OF INTERNET PORNOGRAPHY

#1: The Physical Effects of Pornography

One physical effect of pornography is that the viewer grows to crave more. People aren't satisfied with one image. They want another. The need is to see that which is more risqué and daring, and it takes more and more to satisfy.

A second physical effect is that it makes the porn viewer want an outlet. At some point the viewer desires more than just viewing pornography, which often leads him to other sins. It also brings about a double life. The individual has the life that everyone sees, but then he has a dark secret life that he doesn't want anyone to know about. That secret life is filled with guilt and shame and often leads to lies to keep it hidden.

Scientists and psychiatrists have concluded that pornography is an addiction like alcohol or drug abuse. Addiction is caused by chemical dependencies within the body and neural pathways through the brain. Somebody asks, "How can that be said about pornography?" A brief discussion of the chemistry of the brain is necessary to answer this question. Drs. Randall F. Hyde and Bernell Christensen have written an article entitled *The Brain Science Behind Internet Pornography Addiction*, which was published in January 2010. The following is an explanation of the neurochemicals released in the brain during the use of Internet pornography based on the work of these two experts in this field.

During the process of porn use, there are certain neurochemicals that are released. The first one we will discuss is called **dopamine**. This particular chemical affects the brain so that it very accurately focuses attention and energy. It causes people to ignore negatives. It triggers feelings of ecstasy and creates a powerful dependency. In a healthy marriage relationship, this is a good thing because it causes the couple to focus completely on each other and ignore the negatives. When using pornography, however, it is different. The person's attention is focused on the images. He isn't thinking about his wife, family, beliefs, or consequences; all those are blocked out. And when this chemical is released it creates a chemical dependency that is linked to these images. It is so powerful that it has been directly compared to cocaine addiction. Since it was the pornographic images that produced the feelings, the brain desires those images again and again.

A second chemical released when viewing pornography is **norepinephrine**. Whatever is being experienced when this chemical is released, the smallest details of that experience are seared in the brain as if with a branding iron. In the healthy marriage relationship, wonderful details of the intimate experience are remembered and recalled with fondness, bringing the couple closer together. During porn use, the release of norepinephrine causes the brain to remember the tiniest details of every sexually explicit image. As a result of this chemical, a man can recall in great detail pictures he saw years ago. Those images are seared into his memory. As one man said, "I'm still plagued with what I saw in high school."

The third chemical released is **oxytocin**, a.k.a. "the cuddle chemical." It was first discovered in the brains of mothers while holding their newborn children for the first time. It creates a powerful bond between mother and child, and causes the release of milk for nursing. Oxytocin is a "bonding chemical" and is released when people hold hands, embrace, and kiss. During sexual intimacy, oxytocin is released in high quantities, forging a powerful bond.

Chemical Effects

Dopamine - *feelings of ecstasy and creates dependency*
Norepinephrine - *sears details of the experience*
Oxytocin - *creates a powerful emotional bond*

For example, this chemical causes the husband to be powerfully attracted to certain features of his wife. Through normal day-to-day living, as he sees her, he is reminded of his attraction of her, and his feelings of love and commitment grow. He is bonded more and more to her, and their relationship grows ever stronger.

But what happens when oxytocin is released in the brain while viewing pornography? The viewer is bonded to the body type and features of those he is viewing.[9] Imagine being bonded to those fantasy images with the same kind of power that a newborn child is bonded to his mother and father.

#2: The Marital Effects of Pornography

Sometimes people will try to justify pornography in the marriage and even try to get their spouses to view it with them. The idea that pornography is good for marriage is a lie. The marital consequences are severe. The effects that pornography can have on marriage are devastating. For one, it desensitizes the viewer to his or her own spouse. Porn stars are young, slim, and beautiful. Very few spouses can  compete with such a fantasy. Viewing this makes a person dissatisfied with his spouse. When a person has an "imperfect" spouse, the solution is to look for someone else.

Secondly, pornography hurts the self-esteem of the spouse. In a marriage relationship, it is crushing to the wife that she doesn't satisfy her husband. She wonders what is wrong with her. Pornography puts a wall within the marriage that should never be there. It creates dissatisfaction on the part of the husband and a deep hurt and betrayal on the wife's part. When somebody tries to say that pornography is good for marriage, that's the Devil talking.

#3: The Financial Effects of Pornography

Each year, 12 billion dollars are spent in the United States alone on the sex industry. Where is that money coming from? All too often it's coming from fathers who are using money that ought to be going toward supporting their families! Consider also the cost to businesses. It is estimated that five billion dollars of work hours are lost to cyberporn in the United States.[10] As mentioned earlier, 70 percent of all Internet porn traffic occurs during the nine-to-five workday. Nearly one out of three companies has terminated an employee for inappropriate web use. Not all has been porn, but porn has been a part.[5] *Businessweek* printed the results of a survey stating that 44 percent of U.S. workers with an Internet connection admitted to accessing an X-rated website at work in the month of March 2004.[2]

#4: The Spiritual Effects of Pornography

This is the most important consideration. The use of Internet pornography puts a wall between the viewer and God. Of course,

this is true of any sin that one allows to linger in his life. It hinders his prayers and blocks his worship. First Peter 3:12 says, "For the eyes of the Lord are upon His righteous, and His ears are open to their prayers; but the face of the Lord is against those who do evil." The psalmist wrote in Psalm 66:18, "If I regard iniquity in my heart, the Lord will not hear." When a person allows himself to indulge in the sin of pornography, he is actively building a wall between himself and the God of heaven.

Secondly, some will not obey the gospel (or aren't faithful to the church) because they think they can't quit pornography. They have fallen for the lie that they just can't stop, and they understand there is no point to being a Christian if they are going to live in sin, so they just don't bother to try. Daily they risk their souls living in this condition.

Thirdly, pornography corrupts the heart. Proverbs 23:7 says, "For as he thinketh in his heart, so is he." If a person thinks corrupt thoughts, then he is a corrupt. If one continually fills his mind with filth and smut, so is he. The spiritual implications of this are tragically disturbing.

Fourth, there is the danger of hardening one's heart. Years of viewing pornography can harden a man's conscience. First Timothy 4:2 speaks of those who have had their consciences seared, that is, they have become numb to sin. There is the ever-present danger that an individual can engage in the use of porn—or any sin, for that matter—for so long that it doesn't bother him anymore. This is very dangerous territory, as he may be going down a road of no return, spiritually speaking. Hebrews 6:4 discusses some who had reached a point where it was impossible to renew them to repentance. Don't be one of those people!

PORNOGRAPHY: WHY IT'S WRONG

First and foremost, pornography is a direct violation of Scripture. Ephesians 5:3 (KJV) says, "But fornication and all uncleanness or covetousness, let it not even be named among you, as is fitting for saints." Another version says, "But among you there must not even be a hint of sexual immorality, or of any kind of impurity, or of greed, because these are improper for God's holy people."

In Matthew 5:28, Jesus said, "But I say to you that whoever looks at a woman to lust for her has already committed adultery with her in his heart." Viewing pornography is a direct violation of the Scriptures.

As a point of clarification, sometimes when people read Matthew 5:28 they begin to wonder if pornography is a valid reason for divorce. A woman might reason this way: "I caught my husband viewing pornography. In Matthew 5:28 Jesus equated this to adultery, and since adultery is a scriptural reason for divorce, then I can divorce my husband for viewing pornography."

It's obvious why someone might reason this way, but the conclusion is not correct. Matthew 19:9 gives only one scriptural reason for divorce, and that is fornication. This word means unlawful sexual intercourse. Viewing pornography doesn't fit that definition. When one views pornography, Jesus said he commits adultery in his heart (mind). The spiritual consequences may be the same, but the physical consequences are not.

Let's illustrate this. First John 3:15 says, "Whoever hates his brother is a murderer, and you know that no murderer has eternal life abiding in him." If a man hates his brother in his heart, he is a murderer in the eyes of God, but he won't be taken to jail because of his hate. He won't receive the death penalty. However, the **spiritual** consequences will be the same as if he had really killed his brother. Jesus said, "No murderer has eternal life."

In a similar sense, looking at pornography is adultery of the heart, but it isn't the actual physical act of adultery. Thus,

Violation of Scripture

Pornography is a direct violation of Jesus' words in Matthew 5:28,

"whoever looks at a woman to lust for her has already committed adultery with her in his heart."

Chapter 8

viewing pornography is not grounds for a divorce. It may lead there. It may stimulate a person's desires to the point that he has sex with someone other than his wife, at which point he **will have** committed adultery.

Secondly, pornography is a form of stealing. Someone might think this a strange point to make, but consider the defintion of the word *steal:* "to take (the property of another) without right or permission."[11]

When a man and woman get married, the rights to each other's bodies become those of the spouse. The wife's body belongs to her husband. Any pleasure or enjoyment of a sexual nature that might come from her body belongs only to him. First Corinthians 7:2-4 says, "Let each man have his own wife, and let each woman have her own husband. The wife does not have authority over her own body, but the husband does. And likewise the husband does not have authority over his own body, but the wife does." That being the case, when a man views pornography, he is using or taking that which is not his to take. In essence, he is "taking without right or permission." That is the definition of stealing. He is taking that which belongs only to her husband.

Hebrews 13:4 says, "Marriage is honorable among all, and the bed undefiled; but fornicators and adulterers God will judge." Outside the marriage relationship, a man is not permitted to view or touch a woman in this way. To do so is sin. *Inside* the

bonds of marriage, all the pleasures of the sexual relationship are the husband's and wife's to enjoy. Proverbs 5:18-19 says that a man is to be satisfied with his own wife, and that her breasts should satisfy him at all times. The Bible uses this type of language only with regard to the marriage relationship.

Pornography also steals time that ought to be used for other things. Many porn addicts spend countless hours involved in this sin. A man who uses pornography often neglects spending time with his family, choosing rather to hide behind a locked door perusing porn sites.

His spiritual developent also suffers as his time is consumed with sin rather than good and holy things.

Thirdly, pornography corrupts the heart. Matthew 12:35 says, "A good man out of the good treasure of his heart brings forth good things, and an evil man out of the evil treasure brings forth evil things." If a person is filling his heart with filth, filth is going to come out in his life.

Fourthly, pornography is wrong because it contributes to many other sins. Some of the sins may be physical. It may lead to adultery. It will most certainly lead to lying and cover-ups.

OVERCOMING THE SIN OF PORNOGRAPHY

Overcoming pornography must start with a strong desire. The power that pornography has over men (especially) is very great. When the addiction factor is added and brain chemistry is considered, the task cannot be accomplished without a very strong desire to stop! That desire ought to be present when one considers the fact that he cannot continue to indulge in pornography and go to heaven.

Why It's Wrong
- Violates Scripture
- Form of Stealing
- Corrupts The Heart
- Contributes to other Sins

In addition to the strong desire, a man must also have an equally strong determination. This fight cannot be entered in a half-hearted manner. He cannot wean himself of the desire; he simply has to stop. He must make a covenant with himself like Job did. Job said, "I have made a covenant with my eyes; why then should I look upon a young woman?" (Job 31:1). He made an agreement with his eyes not to look at a woman lustfully.

Somebody asks, "How can a man do that? Immodesty is everywhere!" In the book, *Every Young Man's Battle*, the authors suggest the practice of "bouncing your eyes,"[7] that is, as soon as you see something you shouldn't, train yourself to bounce your eyes onto something else. The point is to avoid things that stimulate sinful desires within you. One of the authors said sometimes when driving, a woman jogging alongside the road would start his mind in the wrong direction. He would immediately "bounce his eyes" elsewhere. For someone else, the temptation might come in a different form. Stimuli are different for every person, but the remedy is the same. It starts with controlling one's heart. It is important to know what is a stumbling block for **you** and not to let your mind linger on it.

With regard to the Internet, icons popping up on the screen might entice you. It is important to make a covenant with  yourself: "I will not visit those sites anymore." That strong determination is absolutely, positively necessary in order to overcome the sin of pornography.

Thirdly, to overcome pornography, it is important to pray and study. Philippians 4:13 says, "I can do all things through Christ Who strengthens me." There is power in the Lord, and we need to ask for it. Especially when faced with temptation, we need to stop and pray. Psalm 119:11 says, "Thy word have I hid in mine heart, that I might not sin against Thee." Studying the Bible and hiding it deep in your heart will help you resist temptation.

Another good weapon to help defeat the addiction of pornography is to have an accountability partner. Overcoming this sin is very hard to do alone. Having someone to "answer to" could mean the difference in success and failure. It should be someone you trust. He will hold you accountable by checking in and asking for updates on your progress.

Somebody might ask, "Where do you find the idea of an accountability partner in the Bible?" James 5:16 says, "Confess your trespasses to one another, and pray for one another, that you may be healed. The effective, fervent prayer of a righteous man avails much." Galatians 6:2 says, "Bear one another's burdens, and so fulfill the law of Christ."

The burden is much lighter when a Christian brother can help you through it. There is even online accountability where a person can have all of his online activity recorded and automatically emailed to a friend of his choosing. One such service is called *Covenant Eyes*. Their software blocks objectionable sites and sends reports of Internet surfing to the person selected to receive the reports. That is a form of what we are suggesting, an accountability partner.

Next, to overcome Internet pornography, eliminate the sources. First Corinthians 6:18 tells us to "flee sexual immorality." Get away from it, or get it away from you! If having your computer in your basement is a stumbling block, move it into the kitchen where everyone can see you when you're using it. Eliminate the temptation. One man said he got hooked on pornography through

How To Overcome It
- Strong Desire
- Strong Determination
- Prayer
- Accountability Partner
- Eliminate Sources
- Change Habits

his job. He monitored Internet traffic, and in seeing what others were looking at, he got pulled in himself. What should one do in a situation like that? Quit the job or ask for a transfer. It sounds radical, but isn't that the point of Matthew 5:29? Jesus said, "If your right eye causes you to sin, pluck it out and cast it from you; for it is more profitable for you that one of your members perish, than for your whole body to be cast into hell." It may be that in your home, you need to buy some software which prevents you from accessing pornographic websites. Give the code to a friend or family member, so only he can make changes.

Finally, change your habits. For many people, viewing Internet pornography is a habit in which they have ensnared themselves. We humans are creatures of habit. Find something else to occupy your time. Rearrange your day, your schedule, or the people with whom you are spending time. Whatever is leading you down this path, change it!

"SEXTING"

Sexting is a word that comes from combining the words, "sex" and "texting." Sexting is one of the latest crazes. Most cell phones have the ability to take pictures and send them to other cell phones. It has become very popular for kids to take pictures of themselves unclothed and to text it to other kids, maybe to a boyfriend or girlfriend. Recently we've even seen scandals as politicians and celebrities have gotten caught up in this fad. Sexting is nothing more than a form of homemade

pornography. Parents may monitor their children's Internet usage. Some even put blocks, filters, and restrictions on the computer, but what about their phones? Some parents may think, "I can't check on things like that. That would be an invasion of their privacy. That's his phone, his computer, his room." The parent with that philosophy is making a huge mistake. God has entrusted the raising of children to parents, and He will also hold them accountable. A parent might think privacy is very important, but the child's soul is far more important.

CONCLUSION

While studying about porn addiction, one will run across many personal stories of disaster. He'll read about lives that were ruined, jobs lost, marriages destroyed, homes wrecked and countless hours wasted. One man explained that during one year he spent over a thousand hours just viewing Internet pornography. When asked what happened to his family, he said, "I lost it." What about his job? He said, "I lost it too...I've lost everything."[12] Imagine losing your family, your job, and finally your eternal soul to a devil's hell, all for the temporary pleasure of pornography. It doesn't have to be that way! Do as Job did; make a covenant with your eyes and start today with a new life.

Video Resources

THE TRUTH ABOUT... PORNOGRAPHY

This video covers the exploding pornography industry. Can Christians engage in viewing pornography?

TheTruthAbout.net/video/Pornography

MARRIAGE DIVORCE & REMARRIAGE

In 2000, the United States Census Bureau predicted that 50 percent of all marriages taking place that year would eventually end in divorce. This epidemic of divorce has caused serious problems not only for our society, but also for the Lord's church. Faithful elderships are constantly having to deal with this heart-wrenching issue, and Christians seeking to teach others sometimes feel they have hit a brick wall when the word *divorce* enters the conversation. Though at times it feels like we do a great deal of teaching on this subject, maybe it's not enough in light of how prevalent the problem really is.

In this study, we will present a very basic outline of what God has to say on the subject of marriage, divorce, and remarriage, and then deal with some errors related to this issue.

The most straightforward and clear passage in the Bible on the subject of marriage, divorce, and remarriage is in Matthew 19. Let's consider it together, starting with verse 1: "Now it came to pass, when Jesus had finished these sayings, that He departed from Galilee and came to the region of Judea beyond the Jordan. And great multitudes followed Him, and He healed them there. The Pharisees also came to Him, testing Him, and saying to Him, 'Is it lawful for a man to divorce his wife for just any reason?'"

The Pharisees had come to Jesus with the intention of testing Him. Their question did not stem from a pure motive. They wanted only to trap Jesus in His words. The Jews of Jesus' day were greatly divided on the question of marriage and divorce, and they hoped to use this against Jesus. Many people today are still divided on this question. But it is worth noting that there was and is a right answer to the marriage/divorce question.

There were two schools of thought among the Jewish leaders of Jesus' day. One line of thought came from the school of Hillel, a Jewish rabbi. He taught that a man could divorce his wife for any reason, whether it be for the slightest offense or even if he simply disliked her personality or manners. That opinion was based on Deuteronomy 24:1, which says, "If then she finds no favor in his eyes" he may give her a bill of divorcement.

The other line of thought was from the school of Shammai. His followers believed that a man could divorce his wife only in the case of adultery. Their reasoning was based on the same passage of Scripture, Deuteronomy 24:1, but on the section that says, "because he has found some uncleanness in her," he may put her away. They interpreted this *uncleanness* to refer to adultery. So these Pharisees came to Jesus, not looking for the truth but hoping to trap Jesus. They wanted to turn one of the groups against Him, so they asked, "Is it lawful for a man to divorce his wife for just any reason?" The King James Version says "for every cause."

Matthew 19:4, "And He answered and said to them, 'Have you not read that He who made them at the beginning 'made them male and female,' and said, *'For this reason a man shall leave his father and mother and be joined to his wife, and the two shall become one flesh?'* So then, they are no longer two but one flesh. Therefore what God has joined together, let not man separate."

MATTHEW 19:4
And He answered and said to them, "Have you not read that He who made them at the beginning 'made them male and female'…"

Notice from verse 4 that Jesus asks the Pharisees, "Have you not read … ?" They came to Him asking a question about marriage and divorce, and Jesus went back to the source of authority, which is the written Word of God. That seems like the obvious thing to do, but many today do not do that. Most people today turn to everything except the Bible to make decisions concerning marriage.

A man called the church building one day and spoke to the preacher. The man was getting married for the fourth time, and wanted the preacher to perform the wedding. Knowing that the man did not have a scriptural right to be married, the preacher declined. The man protested, "But you don't understand! This woman is a good woman!" Apparently in his reasoning the fact that she was a "good woman" made everything okay.

Jesus did not, however, appeal to emotions, or strange reasoning or feelings. Jesus simply said, "Have you not read, that He which made them at the beginning made them male and female." *At the beginning.* Think back in your mind to the beginning, if you will.

Adam was alone in the garden of Eden. Genesis 2:15 says, "Then the LORD God took the man and put him in the garden of Eden to tend and keep it." Verse 18 says, "And the LORD God said, 'It is not good that man should be alone; I will make him a helper comparable to him.'" Beginning in verse 21, "And the LORD God caused a deep sleep to fall on Adam, and he slept; and He took one of his ribs and closed up the flesh in its place. Then the rib which the LORD God had taken from man He made into a woman, and He brought her to the man. And Adam said: 'This is now bone of my bones and flesh of my flesh; she shall be called Woman, because she was taken out of Man.'" This is the event that Jesus is pointing back to when the Pharisees came asking Him about divorce.

> **MATTHEW 19:6**
> So then, they are no longer two but one flesh. Therefore what God has joined together, let not man separate.

Continuing in Matthew 19:6, Jesus said, "So then, they are no longer two but one flesh." Sometimes the question arises: When are two people actually married? Are they truly married at the conclusion of the wedding ceremony, or is it the sexual union that constitutes a marriage?

The answer to this question absolutely must be that, when the ceremony is finished and the marriage license is signed, a man and woman are married. Otherwise, as a man and woman go to spend their first night together on their honeymoon, they are not even husband and wife! It would also mean that everything leading up to the sexual act itself would be sinful. Jesus said, "They are no longer two but one flesh. Therefore what God has joined together, let not man separate." It is very interesting that the Pharisees came to Jesus asking, "For what reason can a man divorce his wife?" and Jesus' answer was "Don't divorce." He said, "What God has joined together let not man separate." The Pharisees might have thought, "All right, we have caught him now. He said don't divorce, but Moses said it was okay."

This brings us to the controversy. Matthew 19:7, "They said to Him, 'Why then did Moses command to give a certificate of divorce, and to put her away?' He said to them, 'Moses, because of the hardness of your hearts, permitted you to divorce your wives, but from the beginning it was not so.'" Jesus is stating that when God designed the home, and institution of marriage, He never intended for it to be corrupted as men have done. God never intended for men to grow tired of their wives and put them away. He never intended adultery or fornication to occur. Men brought about this corruption, and Moses suffered (tolerated) divorce because of the hardness of their hearts. But, this was not the way it was supposed to be from the beginning.

THE EXCEPTION TO THE RULE

Matthew 19:9, Jesus said, "Whoever divorces his wife, except for sexual immorality, and marries another, commits adultery; and whoever marries her who is divorced commits adultery."

Let's restate what Jesus is saying here. Jesus is saying that he who divorces his wife and remarries another commits adultery. This is the rule: He who divorces his wife for any reason and marries somebody else commits adultery. Now Jesus gives one exception to the rule. The exception is, if he divorces her **because of fornication**. The New King James Version says "sexual immorality," but that is not the best translation of the original Greek word. Sexual immorality could refer to the viewing of pornography or lust of the heart. That is not the meaning of the original word. The Greek word here is *porneia*. It refers to "illicit sexual intercourse." The King James Version more accurately

THE EXCEPTION
Matthew 19:9 - "Unless he puts her away for *pornea*"

PORNEA = Fornication, Sexual Intercourse

translates *porneia* as "fornication." This word includes a wide range of things. Certainly it includes adultery, homosexuality, and bestiality. Fornication is the only exception Jesus made which would allow a man to divorce his wife and remarry another without sinning.

Now let us apply the rule. For the sake of example, suppose a man and woman in the first century get married. A few years down the road, the man decides to divorce his wife. Later, he wants to marry another woman. How would the man know whether he has the right to remarry? He simply needs to ask himself, "Do I fit into the exception of Matthew 19:9? Am I an individual who has put away my spouse on the basis of her fornication?" If the answer is no, then this man cannot remarry without becoming an adulterer.

What if the reason the man divorced his wife was incompatibility? Suppose he said, "We just can't get along together; therefore I am divorcing her." Could he remarry? The answer no, he did not meet the exception of Matthew 19:9.

What if he divorced his wife because he didn't love her anymore? That is one of the popular reasons given for divorce in our modern day. Could he remarry? No! That does not meet the exception of Matthew 19:9.

Someone might argue, "Well, that sounds awfully strict." Apparently, the Lord's disciples thought the same thing. In Matthew 19:10 they said, "If such is the case of the man with his wife, it is better not to marry." They were essentially saying, "This is really strict. If this is the way it is, maybe a man would do better not to marry."

Those today who say, "I can't believe that God's law would be that strict," or, "I just can't believe the Lord would expect me to live the rest of my life unmarried" need to look at the comments of the Lord's disciples. The disciples recognized that God's law concerning marriage is very strict. Jesus responded to His disciples in verse 11, "All cannot accept this saying."

What does Jesus mean by this statement? Some think He's talking about the law He has just stated pertaining to marriage. The more likely explanation is that He's responding to the disciples' statement. They basically said, "Hey, if it's this strict, it's better not to get married." Jesus is saying, "That doesn't work for everybody. Not all can accept that." The text of Matthew 19 continues, ". . . but only those to whom it has been given." Some people can take that route. They can remain unmarried. Verse 12, "For there are eunuchs **(people who remain sexually inactive and cannot engage in the intimacies of marriage)** who were born thus from their mother's womb" and, "there are eunuchs who were made eunuchs by men." (This sometimes happened, as in the case of Daniel and others. They were physically maimed so the desire for sexual activity would be taken away.) Finally, "there are eunuchs who have made themselves eunuchs for the kingdom of heaven's sake. He who is able to accept it, let him accept it."

To what does this refer? There are several things involved in Jesus' statement, but certainly at least one of them would include people who have lost the scriptural right to get married, and so for the kingdom's sake, they remain unmarried. They understand the commandment of Matthew 19:9, and so they have no choice but to remain single in order to be right with God.

ERRORS REGARDING MARRIAGE, DIVORCE AND REMARRIAGE

Error #1: Baptism washes away unscriptural marriage.

This false doctrine teaches that if a person entered into an unscriptural (adulterous) marriage before he became a Christian, his adulterous marriage became non-adulterous when he was baptized, and he can remain in that marriage. Someone might argue, "That makes sense because baptism washes away all sins."

But there is one major problem with this: repentance. Before a person can be forgiven of any sin, he must first repent. That is true of stealing, idolatry, lying, homosexuality, and it's true of living in an adulterous marriage. In the eyes of God, a person living in an adulterous marriage is living in constant sin. Every time that man sleeps with his wife, he is committing adultery. In order to be forgiven of that sin, he must stop committing it.

MARRIAGE & DIVORCE

UNSCRIPTURAL MARRIAGE

OBEYING THE GOSPEL IN BAPTISM

Does baptism wash away the sin of a current adulterous marriage?

APPROVED MARRIAGE

Chapter 9

MARRIAGE & DIVORCE

Think of it this way: Suppose there are two men who are "married"—two homosexuals—and they are both baptized. Does baptism change their sinful, homosexual "marriage" into an honorable one? Certainly not! Why not? Because they have not repented. The sin continues. Repentance demands that they stop living in sin.

What about a polygamist marriage? Will baptism transform a polygamist marriage into an honorable one? Again, the answer is no, it will not. Repentance demands that they stop the polygamy. The point here is that repentance demands that the person stop the sin, and certainly adulterous marriage is no exception.

Error #2: Non-Christians are exempt from the Law of Christ.

To summarize, this doctrine argues that Matthew 19 and the laws of marriage are part of God's covenant law for Christians, and so before a person becomes a Christian, God's "covenant" laws don't apply to him. Those holding this doctrine would therefore argue that, if a man enters into an unscriptural marriage before he becomes a Christian, he is not sinning. They would declare him not in violation of Matthew 19. Even if he has been unscripturally married and divorced 10 times before he becomes a Christian, it doesn't matter. He may keep the wife he has at the time of his baptism because, at that moment, they would say God's law concerning marriage begins to apply to him. This is an absolutely false position. God's law applies to everyone. Acts 17:30 says, "Truly, these times of ignorance God overlooked, but now commands **all men everywhere** to repent." This passage teaches that in the past there were things that God overlooked, especially with regard to the Gentiles, but now all men are amenable to the law of Christ.

It is sometimes argued that certain laws apply to Christians, but do not apply to non-Christians. For example, they will cite the command to partake of the Lord's supper. They will say, "The law commanding partcipation in the Lord's Supper is only for those in a covenant relationship with God." They would then argue that the same is true of laws related to marriage; that they only apply to those already in a covenant relationship.

MARRIAGE & DIVORCE

UNSCRIPTURAL MARRIAGE

Does God's law for marriage apply to non-Christians?

APPROVED MARRIAGE

GOD'S LAWS

This is really a silly argument. The truth is that God has commanded all men everywhere to repent and obey the gospel. Then He expects them to engage in all of the appropriate acts of worship that follow.

Just because a man has not yet properly prepared himself does not mean that God's law does not apply to him. This would be like saying that a man who doesn't yet believe is not commanded to be baptized. Most certainly he is! He must first believe, but the command to be baptized has always applied to him.

God's law on marriage applies to all of humanity. First Corinthians 6:9-11 says, "Do you not know that the unrighteous will not inherit the kingdom of God? Do not be deceived. Neither fornicators, nor idolaters, nor **adulterers**, nor homosexuals, nor sodomites, nor thieves, nor covetous, nor drunkards, nor revilers, nor extortioners will inherit the kingdom of God. **And such were some of you**. But you were washed, but you were sanctified, but you were justified in the name of the Lord Jesus and by the Spirit of our God." It is very interesting that these people were viewed as adulterers even before they became Christians. That means God's marriage law applied to them even before they were baptized.

Error #3: If fornication occurs, both parties in the marriage are free to remarry.

This is not what the Bible teaches. It is sometimes argued that if the innocent party—the spouse who did not commit adultery—is freed from the marriage bond and is free to remarry, then the guilty party must also be freed. Proponents of this will say, "If the marriage is dissolved for one, it must of necessity be dissolved for the other."

But Matthew 19:9 is written in such a way as to release the innocent, while binding the guilty. It reads, "Whoever divorces his wife, except for sexual immorality, and marries another, commits adultery; and whoever marries her who is divorced commits adultery." According to this text, only a person who has put away his or her spouse for fornication can remarry. It's as simple as that. The guilty party **has not** put away his spouse

MARRIAGE & DIVORCE

GUILTY PARTY
(Committed adultery
and cannot remarry)

INNOCENT PARTY
(Did not commit adultery
and is free to remarry)

UNSCRIPTURAL
MARRIAGE

APPROVED
MARRIAGE

MATTHEW 19:9

And I say to you, whoever divorces his
wife, except for sexual immorality
(*fornication*) and marries another,
commits adultery; and whoever marries
her who is divorced commits adultery.

for fornication, therefore he cannot remarry. God's law has restricted him in this way.

Verse 9 continues,"and whoever marries her who is divorced commits adultery." So additionally, we learn that if a person has been put away for adultery, he cannot remarry or else he commits adultery. Matthew 19:9 is written to protect the innocent, not to release the guilty. In fact, just imagine the implications if "guilty party doctrine" were true. It would mean that if a man grew tired of his wife, he could cheat on her, so that she would divorce him, and he would then have God's approval to remarry. It means that all an individual would have to do in order to obtain the right to remarry would be to commit adultery. It is absurdity!

Error #4: If children have been conceived in an adulterous marriage, then God desires the home be kept intact and not separated.

Some will argue, "God doesn't want to see a home broken up. God hates divorce. Two wrongs don't make a right." It's true that two wrongs do not make a right, but if a person is living in an unscriptural marriage, that is wrong, but separating from an unscriptural marriage is right. It is never wrong to stop living in sin; in fact, it is required. Matthew 19:9 teaches that people living in adultery cannot continue doing so with God's blessing. Consider this illustration: two people are living in a homosexual marriage, and one of them learns and obeys the gospel. With this newfound knowledge, he understands that he cannot remain in this sinful relationship and be pleasing to God. Divorcing (separating) is not wrong under these circumstances. These individuals cannot continue in that situation and be pleasing to God. The same is true with an unscriptural marriage of a man and woman.

Now what if children were involved? That certainly makes it more difficult from an emotional standpoint, but it does not change the fact of an unscriptural marriage.

The book of Ezra contains an Old Testament example which helps to shed some light on this situation. Under the Law of Moses, God did not permit His people, the Jews, to marry others from the heathen nations. Deuteronomy 7:3 says, "Nor shall you make

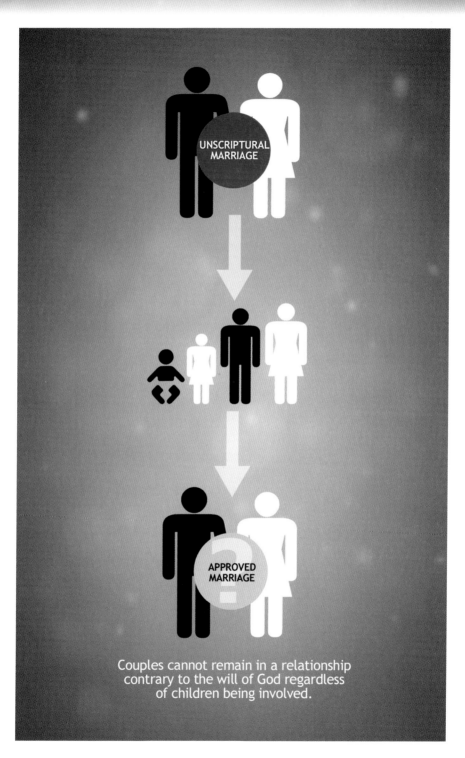

Couples cannot remain in a relationship contrary to the will of God regardless of children being involved.

MARRIAGE & DIVORCE

marriages with them. You shall not give your daughter to their son, nor take their daughter for your son. For they will turn your sons away from following Me, to serve other gods; so the anger of the LORD will be aroused against you." Some of the people ignored God's law. They took for themselves wives of the heathens, and had children with them. But did that change God's law? Read Ezra 10:10-11, "Then Ezra the priest stood up and said to them, 'You have transgressed and have taken pagan wives, adding to the guilt of Israel. Now therefore, make confession to the LORD God of your fathers, and do His will; **separate yourselves** from the peoples of the land, and **from the pagan wives**."

These people could not remain in a relationship contrary to the will of God with His approval, whether children were involved or not. The same goes for people of today. It is true that God hates divorce (Malachi 2:16) when it's the putting away of a scriptural and proper marriage, but that is not our present discussion. We are discussing relationships that never had God's approval in the first place - sinful marriages. God is only pleased when we discontinue sin.

As a side note, when a couple in an unscriptural marriage does right and separates, that does not eliminate their responsibilities toward their children. That daddy still has an obligation to love and support his children.

Error #5: A person in a scriptural marriage may decide to divorce for a reason other than fornication and may do so with God's approval so long as he does not remarry.

This statement is simply not true. When a man and a woman enter into marriage, God joins the two together, and along with the joining comes all of the obligations of marriage. Ephesians 5:25 tells us, "Husbands love your wives." It does not say, "Unless you decide to leave her, and then you can just remain unmarried." First Peter 3:7 says, "Dwell with your wife according to knowledge." Again, it does not say, "Unless you decide to walk away." Ephesians 5:24 and Titus 2:4 command that wives love and be subject to their own husbands. It does not say "unless things get really tough." If an individual decides

MARRIAGE & DIVORCE

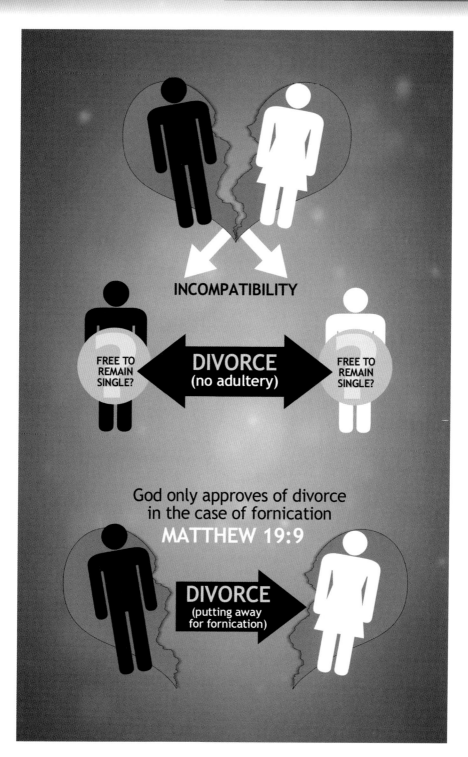

INCOMPATIBILITY

FREE TO REMAIN SINGLE?

DIVORCE
(no adultery)

FREE TO REMAIN SINGLE?

God only approves of divorce
in the case of fornication
MATTHEW 19:9

DIVORCE
(putting away
for fornication)

to simply divorce his or her spouse when no fornication has occurred, that individual is in violation of the aforementioned passages.

First Corinthians 7:10 says, **"Let not the wife depart from her husband**." The English Standard Version says, "To the married I give this charge (not I, but the Lord): **the wife should not separate from her husband**."

A preacher was conducting a study with a family that was contemplating divorce. He pointed out that God only allows divorce for the cause of fornication, at which time one of the family members spoke up and said, "No, the Lord only allows divorce and remarriage for fornication. A couple can divorce if they want to." Such is not the case!

A couple cannot divorce simply because they want to. It is a sin against God. Jesus said, "What therefore **God has joined together let not man separate**." God will not "unjoin" (dissolve) a marriage for a reason other than fornication. He will not sanction a divorce for any other cause. If one is unhappy in his marriage, he cannot simply abandon that marriage and remain single, thinking God is all right with that decision. He will not be. Again, Malachi 2:16 says God hates divorce, and the only time one can get a divorce with God's approval (without sinning) is if one is putting away his spouse on the grounds of fornication.

Error #6: If a person's spouse abandons him or her, then he or she is freed from the marriage and has the right to remarry.

This is absolutely incorrect and is not taught in the Bible. To back up this false statement, some have even cited 1 Corinthians 7:15 as the basis for their argument. Read the passage, noticing the highlighted words, "But if the unbeliever departs, let him depart; a brother or a sister is **not under bondage** in such cases. But God has called us to peace." Some have suggested that here the apostle Paul is giving a second reason for divorcing and remarrying with God's approval, and that is abandonment. The defenders of this view would argue that if one's spouse just runs off, the remaining spouse is at liberty to remarry with God's blessing. They believe that the phrase "not under bondage" suggests that a person is free from the marriage and thus free to remarry.

If that were true, then the phrase "**except** it be for fornication" as stated by Jesus in Matthew 19:9 would be contradicted. Secondly, the very text of 1 Corinthians 7 states the opposite of this. What if one's spouse does leave him? What is his situation? Let 1 Corinthians 7:10-11 answer, "Now to the married I command, yet not I but the Lord: a wife is not to depart from her husband. But even if she does depart, let her remain unmarried or be reconciled to her husband. And a husband is not to divorce his wife."

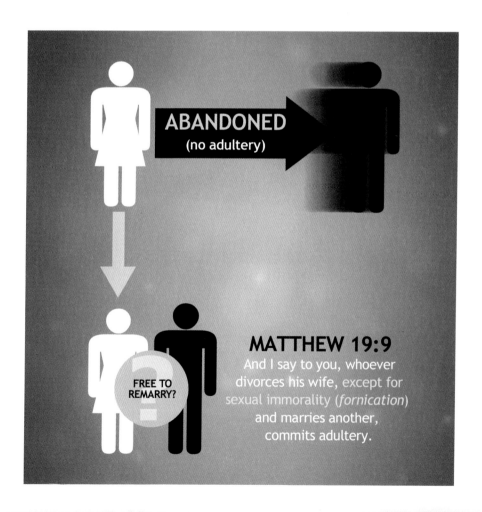

ABANDONED
(no adultery)

MATTHEW 19:9
And I say to you, whoever divorces his wife, except for sexual immorality (*fornication*) and marries another, commits adultery.

FREE TO REMARRY?

God commands the spouse not to leave, but if she sins and does leave, the Lord says, "Do not divorce her." The remaining spouse is still married and is not free to divorce.

What then does 1 Corinthians 7:15 mean? The English Standard Version says, "But if the unbelieving partner separates, let it be so. In such cases the brother or sister is not enslaved. God has called you to peace." Let us paraphrase the meaning: If an individual's unbelieving spouse says, "You quit this Christianity stuff or I'm leaving," then let him or her go. The Christian is not enslaved to his spouse. He must be faithful to the Lord.

CONCLUSION

Not every marriage/divorce scenario is simple. Some are difficult to sort through, but God's basic law is not hard to understand. It says **stay married**. There is only one exception to that law. It is granted as a concession to the innocent, and that is fornication. In the case of fornication, the innocent party may put away his guilty spouse and may remarry with God's approval.

Why does God allow this one exception? Perhaps because He knows how it feels. When we commit spiritual adultery against the Him, He knows how it feels.

Video Resources

MARRIAGE, DIVORCE & REMARRIAGE

 With more than half of marriages ending in divorce, to say that a study of the subject is needed is an understatement. Most people don't know what God has to say about divorce, and many don't care. This video delves into a crucial topic that is affecting the very fabric of our society.

TheTruthAbout.net/video/Marriage-Divorce

What must I do to be SAVED?

"What must I do to be saved?" This is the most important of all questions. It is a question that has implications not only here and now but on into eternity. A million years after you die, the answer to this question will still matter.

But as important as the question is, it is answered wrongly on a daily basis. A person might ask five different people this question and receive five different answers. If we were talking about a less crucial subject, that might be all right. If we were asking, "Which football team is the greatest football team ever?" and got five different answers, that would be okay. If we were discussing which is the best fast food restaurant and received a variety of answers, that would be acceptable, and even expected.

But there is no room for error on the question of our present discussion, because the difference between a wrong answer and right answer is the difference between heaven and hell. What we have to do is go to the Bible, the only source for the right answer to this question.

One might pick up the phone, call a local denomination, and ask the preacher, "What must I do to be saved?" A common answer he might receive is "Say the Sinner's Prayer." Would you be surprised to learn that this so-called "Sinner's Prayer" is not found anywhere in the pages of the Bible? Would you further be surprised to realize that of all the conversion accounts in the New Testament, not one person was saved by prayer? If we're going to be saved today, it is going to have to be the same way they were saved in the New Testament. God's plan of salvation has not changed.

What did God require people to do in New Testament times to be saved from their sins? When we read the New Testament, particularly the book of Acts (the book of conversions) we see absolute consistency. From Acts 2, the day the church began, and forward, everyone was saved the same way. They all went through the same steps. Sometimes we summarize those steps this way: hear, believe, repent, confess, and be baptized. Every person who was saved went through these same steps.

"What did God require people to do in the New Testament to obtain salvation from their sins?"

If we simply left the discussion with this summary though, we would be doing the reader a great disservice. Obviously more explanation is needed. In the next several pages, we will show what a person really needs to know to become a Christian and be saved from his sins.

HEAR

No man can be saved if he does not hear the gospel. Romans 10:13-14 says, "Whoever calls on the name of the LORD shall be saved. How then shall they call on Him in whom they have not believed? And how shall they believe in Him of Whom they have not heard? And how shall they hear without a preacher?"

And how shall they believe in Him of whom they have not heard? And how shall they hear without a preacher?

ROMANS 10:14

This passage teaches that it is necessary to call on the name of the Lord in order to be saved; it is necessary to believe in order to call; it is necessary to hear in order to believe. And so, a man who never hears the gospel cannot be be saved. That is why the verse goes on to say, "And how shall they hear without a preacher?" In other words, those who are already Christians had better spread the gospel or else people will be lost!

SAVED?

Someone asks, "What about those who never hear the gospel? Will they still be condemned even though they were ignorant of the truth?" Acts 17:30 says, "Truly, these times of **ignorance** God overlooked, but now commands **all men everywhere** to repent, because He has appointed a day on which He will judge the world."

The point is that ignorance is not an excuse. Someone might protest, "Are you saying that people are going to be lost because of ignorance?" No, people are going to be lost because of sin. The problem is that ignorance cannot wash away sins; only the blood of Christ can do that. And so, if a person is going to be saved, the process must begin with him hearing about the blood of Christ. If a man doesn't hear the gospel, he may go through life never knowing that his sins have caused him to lose his soul. Romans 6:23 says, "For the wages of sin is death (eternal death), but the gift of God is eternal life in Christ Jesus our Lord." A man may never know he is destined for eternity in hell, and by not knowing, he is certainly not going to do anything about his situation. Thus, he must hear about the problem. Once he's realized the problem,

> For the wages of sin is death, but the gift of God is eternal life in Christ Jesus our Lord.
>
> **ROMANS 6:23**

he certainly needs to hear the remedy also. It does no good for someone to know he is lost unless he knows what to do about it, so he must hear the remedy.

When God created man in the Garden of Eden, man was sinless and in perfect fellowship with God. But it wasn't long until mankind sinned. This created a very serious problem because inherent in the nature of God is **justice**. Psalm 89:14 says, "Righteousness and justice are the foundation of Your throne." Perhaps one of the greatest misunderstandings people have of God is the belief that He can simply choose to overlook sin if He so desires. Sometimes people say, "God won't let that lone person in the jungles of South America who has never heard the gospel be lost! Surely He'll save them anyway!" The truth however is that God cannot simply choose to overlook sin. In fact, if God were to ignore even one single sin, He would at that point cease to be a just God. He would no longer be a God of righteousness and perfection.

Leviticus 24:17-20 lays down the principle of justice: an eye for an eye, a tooth for a tooth, a breach for a breach, and a life for a life. Justice requires a life for a life. The very nature of God demands it. This is not an optional matter. Justice has to be served. The penalty for sin has to be paid. Now, God could have allowed man to pay the penalty himself and die, but His love for us longed for another way. There was only one other way, and that was for God Himself to pay it. Thus God arranged a plan to pay that price for every person. He sent Christ—a member of the godhead—to become a human being, born of a virgin, to live a perfect life and die in our place. Isaiah 53:5 says, "But He was wounded for our transgressions, He was bruised for our iniquities; the chastisement for our peace was upon Him, and by His stripes we are healed."

A individual cannot be saved if he doesn't hear these things. Every person in the Bible who became a Christian first heard the gospel. No hearing equals no hope.

BELIEVE

Upon hearing the gospel, a man must believe it. Specifically, what must the sinner believe? He must believe what he has heard! Mark 16:15-16 says, "And He said to them, 'Go into all the world and preach the gospel to every creature. He who **believes** and is baptized will be saved, but he who does not **believe** will be condemned.'" Clearly the Bible states that an individual must believe in order to be saved, but what does this entail? First, a man must understand **that Jesus is the Christ, the Son of God**. In John 8:24, Jesus said, "If you do not believe that I am He, you will die in your sins." Man must understand that He, Jesus, is deity. John 1:14 tells us, "And the Word became flesh and dwelt among us, and we beheld His glory, the glory as of the only begotten of the Father, full of grace and truth."

Secondly, a man must believe in the **death, burial, and resurrection of Jesus Christ**; that while we were yet sinners

SAVED?

Christ died for us (Romans 5:8) and then arose from the grave, defeating death (1 Corinthians 15:54-55). Romans 10:9 says, "If you confess with your mouth the Lord Jesus and believe in your heart that God has raised Him from the dead, you will be saved."

It is also crucial that we believe and understand **the body of Christ**. The Bible teaches that salvation is found only in Christ's body. Second Timothy 2:10 says that salvation is in Christ, and 1 John 5:11 says, "God has given us eternal life, and this life is in His Son." Sometimes there exist people who have been baptized into Christ, but they still seem to think that one church is as good as another. They will come out of the watery grave of baptism and be offended at the idea that denominationalism is sinful. When this happens, clearly they have failed to receive essential information.

Salvation
The Bible clearly teaches that salvation is found only in the "one body" of Christ.

The Bible plainly teaches that salvation is found only in the "one body" of Christ (Ephesians 4:4), and it is vital that every person understands that fact in order to be saved. How can one be saved in the one body of Christ if he has never been taught about that one body?

In Acts 8 Philip went down to the city of Samaria and preached the gospel. Verse 12 says, "But when they believed Philip as he preached the things **concerning the kingdom** of God and the name of Jesus Christ, both men and women were baptized." Note this: Philip taught those people about the kingdom of God, which is the one church of the Bible. Philip taught them, and when they believed what they heard, they were baptized. Belief in the one body of Christ is an essential part of the plan.

As a side note, the text says, men and women were baptized. Never in the Bible do we read about little children being baptized, and indeed they don't need to be. Those who are accountable in the eyes of God are those who have reached a certain level of mental development. They must be old enough to believe.

First Corinthians 12:12-13 say, "For as the body is **one**, and hath many members, and all the members of that **one body**, being many, are **one body**, so also is Christ. For by one Spirit are we all baptized into **one body**." This passage teaches that there is one body. (Ephesians 1:22-23 says the body is the church.) We are therefore baptized into the one body of Christ, which is His one church. How could a person be taught the gospel without being informed of that fundamental truth?

This is the second step of the plan of salvation. A person must believe in the diety of Christ, His death, burial, and resurrection and the one body wherein are the saved.

REPENT

This third step in gospel plan of salvation was first taught in the Christian Age in Acts 2. Those present on the day of Pentecost wanted to know the answer to the very question we are discussing, "What must I do to be saved?" Verse 37 says, "They cried out, 'Men and brethren, what shall we do?'" Peter answers them in verse 38, "Repent, and let every one of you be baptized in the name of Jesus Christ for the remission of sins."

Repentance includes three things. First, it is **a change of mind.** Matthew 21:28-29 illustrates repentance very well. It says, "But what do you think? A man had two sons, and he came to the first and said, 'Son, go, work today in my vineyard.' He said, 'I will not,' but afterward he **repented** [regretted] and went." The son had a change of mind. This is repentance.

Some think *repentance* simply means "to stop sinning," but there are a couple of problems with that idea. First, the discontinuation of the sin follows repentance (the change of mind), it is not the repentance itself. Secondly, a person could stop sinning without ever repenting if he stopped for the wrong reason.

This brings us to the second aspect of repentance: **godly sorrow.** Second Corinthians 7:10 says, "For godly sorrow produces repentance leading to salvation, not to be regretted; but the sorrow of the world produces death." What causes that change of mind known as repentance? Godly sorrow; sorrow for sinning against God and jeopardizing one's eternal soul.

SAVED?

Thirdly, repentance involves **a change of life.** Sometimes this is called the "fruit of repentance." In other words, if an individual has repented in his mind, others should be able to see that repentance in his life. For example, if godly sorrow causes someone to repent of stealing, that person will not be stealing anymore. He has had a change of life. Repentance is a change of mind produced by godly sorrow, resulting in a change of life. Acts 17:30 says, "Truly, these times of ignorance God overlooked, but now commands all men everywhere to repent."

CONFESS

Fourth, confession is necessary for salvation. Romans 10:10 says, "For with the heart one believes unto righteousness, and with the mouth **confession is made unto salvation**." In Acts 8, as Philip was teaching the gospel to the Ethiopian eunuch, he said, "See, here is water. What hinders me from being baptized?" Philip responded, "If you believe with all your heart, you may." And the eunuch answered, **"I believe that Jesus Christ is the Son of God"** (Acts 8:37). With his mouth, he made the good confession. This is the confession we are talking about; confession of what one believes.

Sometimes people mistakenly think that they have to confess all their sins when they become Christians. Imagine how much confessing a 40-year-old would have to do to become a Christian. That's a lot of confessing! No one could do it.

The steps of the plan of salvation are a very natural progression. One must hear the gospel, and believe it, which leads to changing one's mind (or repenting). Then the person verbalizes (confesses) that he believes what he has heard.

Occasionally when talking about the confession, people reference Matthew 10:32-33 where Jesus said, "Therefore whoever confesses Me before men, Him I will also confess before My Father Who is in heaven. But whoever denies Me before men, him will I also deny before My Father Who is

SAVED?

in heaven." This is not really a proper verse to use to teach confession as a step of the plan of salvation. Although the principle of confession is here, this verse is not specifically talking about the good confession; This was said to the apostles in what we call the Limited Comission. It was said to encourage them as they went out to preach.

BE BAPTIZED

Finally, in order to be saved one must be baptized to have his sins washed away. In Acts 22:16, Ananias said to Saul, "And now why are you waiting? Arise and **be baptized**, and wash away your sins, calling on the name of the Lord."

A person cannot be saved until his sins are washed away, and Acts 22:16 teaches that sins are washed away in baptism. This means one cannot be saved first and then baptized later, as is commonly taught by many in denominations. Acts 2:38 says, "Repent, and let every one of you **be baptized** in the name of Jesus Christ for the remission of sins." One cannot have his sins remitted before he is baptized; therefore, one is not saved until he is baptized.

What washes sins away? The blood of Jesus Christ! In Matthew 26:28, Jesus said, "For this is my **blood** of the new covenant, which is shed for many for the remission of sins." Revelation 1:5 says that Jesus Christ "loved us and washed us from our sins **with His own blood**." A man cannot be saved until he has been washed in the blood of Jesus.

If we are saved by the blood of Jesus and our sins are washed away by the blood of Jesus, then what role does baptism play? It is in baptism that an individual contacts the blood of Jesus. Jesus shed His blood in His death, and it is in death that we contact it. Romans 6:3-4 says, "Or do you not know that as many of us as were baptized into Christ Jesus **were baptized into His death?** Therefore we were buried with Him **through baptism into death**,

Baptism
Every person in the Bible who became a Christian and was saved was baptized in order to do so.

SAVED?

that just as Christ was raised from the dead by the glory of the Father, even so we also should walk in newness of life." Why is one raised to walk in newness life when he comes out of the water of baptism? The answer is, because he died to sin. In baptism, he is cleansed by the blood of Jesus.

When a person suggests that one may be saved without baptism, he is suggesting that he or she can be saved without the blood of Christ. The reason this is not true is **because baptism is where a man contacts the blood of Christ**. Every person in the Bible who we read about being saved and becoming a Christian was baptized in order to do so. Baptism is **specifically** mentioned in many of the conversion accounts.

- **Day of Pentecost:** Acts 2:38, "Repent and let every one of you be baptized in the name of Jesus Christ for the remission of sin." Acts 2:41, "Then those who gladly received his word were baptized."
- **Ethiopian Eunuch:** Acts 8:36, the eunuch said, "See, here is water. What hinders me from being baptized?" Verse 38, "And both Philip and the eunuch went down into the water, and he baptized him."
- **People of Samaria:** Acts 8:5, "Then Philip went down to the city of Samaria, and preached Christ unto them." Verse 12 says, "But when they believed Philip as he preached the things concerning the kingdom of God and the name of Jesus Christ, both men and women were baptized."
- **Cornelius:** Acts 10:47 describes the conversion of Cornelius and his household, saying, "Peter asked, 'Can anyone forbid water, that these should not be baptized?'"
- **Lydia:** Acts 16 shows the account of Lydia and her conversion to Christ. Verse 15 says, "And when she and her household were baptized, she begged us, saying… "
- **Philippian Jailer:** Acts 16 talks about the Philippian jailer and says in verse 33, "And he took them the same hour of the night and washed their stripes. And immediately he and all his family were baptized."
- **Saul of Tarsus** Acts 22:16 relates the conversion of Saul: "Ananias said to him, 'And now why are you waiting? Arise and be baptized, and wash away your sins, calling on the name of the Lord.'"

The Gospel Enacted

1 Corinthians 15:3-4

Jesus the Christ
His Death, Burial and Resurrection
For the Sins of Man

Resurrection

Death

Burial

SAVED?

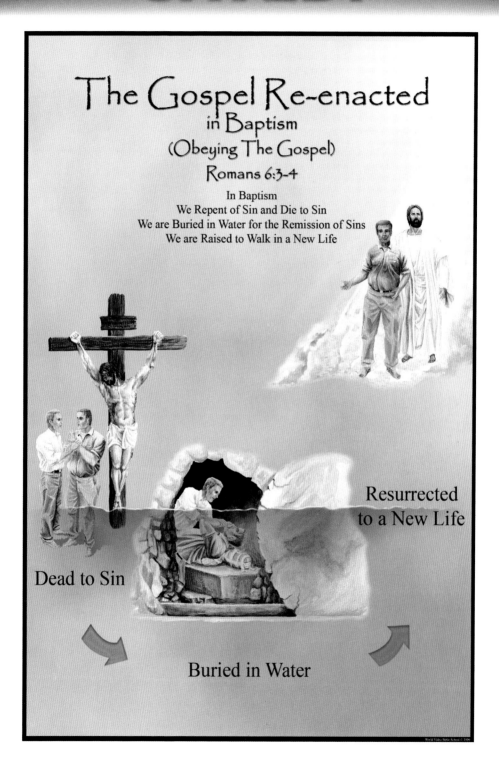

The Gospel Re-enacted
in Baptism
(Obeying The Gospel)
Romans 6:3-4

In Baptism
We Repent of Sin and Die to Sin
We are Buried in Water for the Remission of Sins
We are Raised to Walk in a New Life

Dead to Sin

Buried in Water

Resurrected
to a New Life

SAVED?

Many in the religious world say baptism is not necessary, that a man is saved prior to baptism, and that baptism has nothing to do with salvation, but the Bible tells us in 1 Peter 3:21, "There is also an antitype **which now saves us, baptism** (not the removal of the filth from the flesh, but the answer of a good conscience toward God)."

When discussing the plan of salvation, it's interesting that many freely admit the necessity of hearing the gospel. Most will acknowledge that we must believe. Most also accept repentance. Few arguments are made over the need for confession. But many will deny that baptism is necessary. Notice the conversion accounts chart on the next page. Acts has nine accounts of people obeying the gospel and becoming Christians. It's worthy of notice that all steps of the plan of salvation (hear, believe, repent, confess, and be baptized) are not specifically mentioned in each account. Even though confession is commanded by God in order to be saved, it is not specifically mentioned in most of the accounts of conversion. The same is true of repentance. Few would ever question the necessity of repentance, and certainly the Bible commands it, but it is not always specifically mentioned.

Now notice baptism. In each of these nine accounts, baptism is specifically mentioned. To help us appreciate the necessity and importance of baptism, envision in your mind a circle. Label the circle the "Body of Christ." Next to that circle, envision a stick man. Draw him there in your mind. Second Timothy 2:10 says that salvation is in Christ, so write the word *salvation* in the circle. First John 5:11 says that eternal life is in Christ, so now write *eternal life* inside that circle as well. Now the question of the utmost importance: if salvation is inside that circle, and eternal life is inside that circle, how does one get into the circle? Galatians 3:27 gives us the answer, "For as many of you as were **baptized into** Christ have put on Christ."

Baptism is the doorway. It puts you into Christ, wherein is salvation.

SAVED?

Conversions
in the book of Acts

	HEAR	BELIEVE	REPENT	CONFESS	BAPTISM/SAVED
PENTECOST	Acts 2:14ff	Implied (v.37,41)	Repent (v.37-38)		Taught (v.38) Baptized (v.41)
SAMARIA	Acts 8:5ff	Believed (v.12,13)			Baptized (v.12-13,16)
THE EUNUCH	Acts 8:35-39	Taught & Believed (v.37)		Confessed (v.37)	Baptized (v.38)
SAUL	Acts 9;22;26	Implied (9:6;22:10)	Implied (9:9,11)	Implied (9:6;22:10)	Taught (22:16) Baptized (9:18)
CORNELIUS	Acts 10-11	Taught (10:43)	Implied (11:18)		Commanded (10:47-48)
LYDIA	Acts 16:13	Implied (v.14)			Baptized (v.15)
THE JAILER	Acts 16:31ff	Taught (v.31)			Baptized (v.33)
CORINTHIANS	Acts 18:8	Believed (v.8)			Baptized (v.8)
EPHESIANS	Acts 19:1ff	Taught (v.4)			Baptized (v.5)

COUNTING THE COST

There is one more very important point to be made on this subject. When studying the gospel with someone, it is essential to discuss the cost of becoming a Christian. What is involved in being a Christian?

Many times a person is baptized on a Sunday morning but he doesn't come back to services on Sunday night. He will also be absent on Wednesday night and other times during the week when the church assembles.

SAVED?

At the point of baptism a person is washed from his sins and is saved. Acts 2:47 says that God adds that individual to the church. What about after that? The Bible teaches that every person must hear, believe, repent, confess, be baptized, and **live faithfully**. When a person becomes a Christian, he is giving his life, his all. In Luke 14:27-33, Jesus said, "And whoever does not bear his cross [die to self] and come after Me cannot be My disciple. For which of you, intending to build a tower, does not sit down first and **count the cost**, whether he has enough to finish it—lest, after he has laid the foundation, and is not able to finish, all who see it begin to mock him, saying, 'This man began to build and was not able to finish.' **So likewise, whoever of you does not forsake all that he has cannot be My disciple**."

Becoming a Christian is an absolute commitment. It is a commitment to attend, to give, to worship, to study, to teach. Until a person is ready to give God his all, he is not ready to become a Christian.

Video Resources

WHAT MUST I DO TO BE SAVED?

The answer to this question has implications both now and for eternity. Sadly, wrong answers are being given all the time. With a question of this magnitude, you cannot afford to be wrong.

TheTruthAbout.net/video/Being-Saved

REFERENCES

Chapter 1: Tattoos & Piercings

1. Gorgan, Elena. "New Tattooed Barbie Sparks Outrage with Parents." *Softpedia*. 30 Apr. 2009. Web. <http://news.softpedia.com/news/New-Tattooed-Barbie-Sparks-Outrage-with-Parents-110548.shtml>.
2. "Teenage Skin." *American Academy of Dermatology*. n.d. Web. <http://www.aad.org/media-resources/stats-and-facts/prevention-and-care/teenage-skin>.
3. "Three in Ten Americans with a Tattoo Say Having One Makes Them Feel Sexier." *Harris Interactive*. 12 Feb. 2008. Web. <http://www.harrisinteractive.com/vault/Harris-Interactive-Poll-Research-Three-in-Ten-Americans-with-a-Tattoo-Say-Having-One-Makes-Them-Feel-Sexier-2008-02.pdf>.
4. "Body Art and Tattoos in the Workplace." *FoxNews.com*. 21 Oct. 2006.Web. <http://www.foxnews.com/story/2006/10/21/body-art-and-tattoos-in-workplace/>.
5. "Tattoos: Understand Risks and Precautions." *Mayo Clinic*. n.d. Web. <http://www.mayoclinic.com/health/tattoos-and-piercings/MC00020>.
6. "How Much Does a Tattoo Cost?" *CostHelper Health*. n.d. Web. <http://health.costhelper.com/tattoo.html>.

Chapter 2: Gambling

1. Nadian, Jacob. "Christian Views of Gambling." n.d. Web. <http://www.stmarkscathedral.org/Gambling%20(Lottery%20and%20Gambling).pdf>.
2. Stauffer, Douglas D. "What Is Wrong with Gambling?" *BibleBelievers.com*. n.d. Web. <http://www.biblebelievers.com/stauffer/stauffer_gambling.html>.
3. Jackson, Wayne. "Is Gambling a Moral Issue?" Christian Courier. n.d. Web. <https://www.christiancourier.com/articles/1032-is-gambling-a-moral-issue>.
4. "Probability Of Winning The Lottery - Don't Waste Your Money." *SavingAdvice.com*. n.d. Web. <http://www.savingadvice.com/forums/other/5559-probability-winning-lottery-dont-waste-your-money.html>.
5. "Ask the Wizard: Lottery–FAQ." n.d. Web. <http://wizardofodds.com/ask-the-wizard/lottery>.
6. "How Gaming Benefits Nevada." *Nevada Resort Association*. n.d. Web. <http://www.nevadaresorts.org/benefits/education.php>.

Chapter 3: Drinking

1. "Treatment for Alcohol Abuse." *Remedy Health Media*. 10 Sep 2012. Web. <http://www.healthcommunities.com/alcohol-abuse/treatment.shtml>.
2. "Traffic Safety Facts 2002: Alcohol." *National Highway Traffic Safety Administration*. 2002. Web. <http://www-nrd.nhtsa.dot.gov/Pubs/2002ALCFACTS.PDF>.
3. "Alcohol." *West Seneca Police Department*. 2013. Web. <http://www.wspolice.com/index.php?option=com_content&view=article&id=235&Itemid=157>.
4. "Stop Liquor Ads on TV." *Center for Science in the Public Interest*. Feb 2002. Web. <http://www.cspinet.org/booze/liquorads/liquor_talkingpoints2.htm>.
5. "Teen Drug and Alcohol Safety." *Brattleboro Police Department*. May 2008. Web. <http://www.brattleboropolice.com/safetymay08.html>.
6. "Drinking and Driving Facts." *North Dakota Department of Transportation*. n.d. Web. <http://www.dot.nd.gov/divisions/safety/drinking_driving.htm>.
7. "Alcohol Use and Abuse." *FAQs.org*. n.d. Web. <http://www.faqs.org/health/topics/24/Alcohol-use-and-abuse.html>.
8. Rutherford, Rod. "Woe Unto Them That Drink Strong Drink." *The Power Lectures: Major Lessons From the Major Prophets*. 1995. Print.
9. Jeffcoat, W.D. *The Bible and "Social" Drinking*. Huntsville, Alabama: Publishing Designs. 2006. Print.
10. "Driving Safely by Avoiding Alcohol." *The Journal of the American Medical Association* 283.17 (2000): 2340 (doi:10.1001/jama.283.17.2340).

11. "Red Wine and Resveratrol: Good for Your Heart?" *Mayo Clinic*. 9 Mar 2007. Web. <http://www.faqs.org/health/topics/24/Alcohol-use-and-abuse.html>.
12. Grogan, Martha. "Grape Juice: Same Heart Benefits as Wine?" *Mayo Clinic*. 23 Jul 2011. Web. <http://www.mayoclinic.com/health/food-and-nutrition/AN00576>.
13. Ewing, Charles Wesley. *The Bible and Its Wines*. Denver, Colorado: The National Prohibition Foundation. 1985. Print.

Chapter 4: Dancing

1. "Ratings:'Dancing with the Stars' Premiere Hits All-time High." *Entertainment Weekly*. 10 Mar 2009. Web. <http://insidetv.ew.com/2009/03/10/ratings-dancing-2/>.
2. Humphrey, Sandra. *Don't Kiss Toads*. Nashville, Tennessee: Gospel Advocate Company. 2001. Print.
3. Webster, Allen. *Should Christians Dance?* Jacksonville, Alabama: House to House - Heart to Heart. Print.
4. Hollingworth, Leta S. *The Psychology of the Adolescent*. New York: D. Appleton and Company. 1928. Print.
5. Maxey, Kevin. "Are You Going to the Prom?" 9 Apr 2009. Web. <http://web.archive.org/web/20060515083000/http://www.dcoc.org/sermons/20060409pm.pdf>.
6. "Prom Fashion 2010." *CyberGown.com*. n.d. Web. <http://www.shopshop.com/prom-fashion-2009.html>.
7. "Best Prom Workouts." *PromGirl.net*. n.d. Web. <http://www.promgirl.net/promworkouts.html>.
8. Johnson, Laura. "Top Ten Prom Dance Songs for 2009." Helium.com. 8 Mar 2009. Web. <http://www.helium.com/items/1366902-best-dance-songs-for-prom-2009>.

Chapter 8: Pornography

1. "Statistics." *K9 Web Protection*. n.d. Web. <http://www1.k9webprotection.com/news/files/Online_Safety_Statistics.pdf>.
2. "Porn Statistics: Statistics and Information on Pornography in the USA." *Blazing Grace*. n.d. Web. <http://www.blazinggrace.org/porn-statistics/>.
3. Rovou, Jason. "'Porn & Pancakes' Fights X-rated Addictions." CNN.com. 6 Apr 2007. Web. <http://www.cnn.com/2007/US/04/04/porn.addiction/>.
4. "Internet Pornography Statistics." *TopTenReviews.com*. n.d. Web. <http://internet-filter-review.toptenreviews.com/internet-pornography-statistics.html>.
5. Bissette, David C. "Internet Porn Statistics: 2003." *HealthyMind.com*. n.d. Web. <http://web.archive.org/web/20090810194537/http://healthymind.com/s-porn-stats.html>.
6. "Morality Continues to Decay." *Barna Group*. 3 Nov 2003. Web. <https://www.barna.org/barna-update/article/5-barna-update/129-morality-continues-to-decay>.
7. Arterburn, Stephen, and Fred Stoeker. *Every Young Man's Battle*. Colorado Springs, Colorado: Waterbrook Press. 2009. Print.
8. "Fatal Addiction: Ted Bundy's Final Interview." *PureIntimacy.org*. n.d. Web. <http://www.pureintimacy.org/f/fatal-addiction-ted-bundys-final-interview/>.
9. "Addiction to Porn is a Real Addiction." n.d. Web. <http://www.overcoming-porn-addiction.com/addiction-to-porn.html>.
10. "Internet Porn by the Numbers." *ForYourMarriage.org*. n.d. Web. <http://www.foryourmarriage.org/internet-porn-by-the-numbers/>.
11. "Steal." *TheFreeDictionary.com*. n.d. Web. <http://www.thefreedictionary.com/Stealing>.
12. "Tragic (True) Stories from the Internet." WiseChoice.net. n.d. Web. < http://www.wisechoice.net/addiction-stories/>.

The Truth About... on 🎥 DVD

The Truth About... Moral Issues

The DVD covers in video format eight chapters from this book. **Don Blackwell** presents these lessons addressing today's problems with Bible answers. Each lesson is approximately 30 minutes in length. The lessons include: Gambling; Drinking; Modesty; Lying (part 1 and 2); Pornography; Dancing and Tattoos. These are great teaching lessons for Bible classes from junior high through adult.

Marriage, Divorce and Remarriage

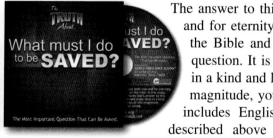

With more than half of marriages ending in divorce, to say that a study of the subject is needed is an understatement. **Don Blackwell** delves into this crucial topic that is affecting the very fabric of our society. If you are considering divorce or you know someone who is, please don't go any further until you watch this video. The DVD includes English subtitles and the lesson interpreted into American Sign Language (ASL) by **Michael Fehmer**.

What Must I Do To Be Saved?

The answer to this question has implications both now and for eternity. In this study, **Don Blackwell** opens the Bible and shares with us God's answer to this question. It is a simple, straight-forward study done in a kind and loving manner. With a question of this magnitude, you can't afford to be wrong. The DVD includes English subtitles and includes the lesson described above as interpreted into American Sign Language (ASL) by **Michael Fehmer**.

All DVDs are available from World Video Bible School®.
Order online at www.WVBS.org or by phone (512-398-5211)

Other Books by WVBS

Would you like the eBook version?

An eBook version is available for most devices from either World Video Bible School's website or the appropriate ebook store for your device.

WVBS.org
Amazon.com
iTunes.com
BN.com

Searching for Truth (Study Guide)

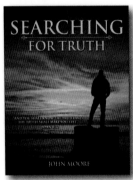

This study guide was written by **John Moore** and is a great resource as a companion to the *Searching for Truth* DVD, or used on its own as a workbook. The material is suitable for individual Bible study or used in any Bible class setting. The text follows the same chapter structure and is nearly a word-for-word transcript of the DVD.

Translations are available in Spanish, Korean, and Swahili.

Men in the Making

Many forces in our culture have declared war on young men. *Men in the Making* is a bold new book by **Kyle Butt, Stan Butt**, and **J.D. Schwartz** to empower young men to be pure, brave, and stand strong against the destructive forces of Satan. This **full-color, 92-page book would benefit every young man from 12 to 20 years old**. In addition, the book is filled with many references to great teaching resources located online (for free) or on other DVDs and books.